The Adventures And MisAdventures Of Peter Beard In Africa

The Adventures And MisAdventures Of Peter Beard In Africa

JON BOWERMASTER

A Bulfinch Press Book   Little, Brown and Company   Boston   New York   Toronto   London

First Edition

The illustrations in this book are reproduced courtesy of the
Peter H. Beard Archive and the following individuals:
Najma Beard, Carol Bell, Jon Bowermaster, Dougie Collins,
Minnie Cushing, Mark Greenberg at Visions Photo, Inc.,
Interview magazine, The Marlborough Gallery, and Peter Riva.

Library of Congress Cataloging-in-Publication Data
Bowermaster, Jon.
    The adventures and misadventures of Peter Beard in Africa / Jon
Bowermaster. — 1st ed.
        p.   cm.
    ISBN 0-8212-1907-3
    1. Beard, Peter H. (Peter Hill), 1938-.   —Journeys—
Kenya—Pictorial works.   2. Photographers—United States—
Biography.   3. Wildlife depredation—Kenya—Pictorial works.
4. Soil degradation—Kenya—Pictorial works.   I. Title.
TR140.B39B68   1993
770'.92—dc20
[B]   92-1821

Bulfinch Press is an imprint and trademark of Little, Brown and Company (Inc.)
Published simultaneously in Canada by Little, Brown & Company (Canada) Limited

PRINTED IN THE UNITED STATES OF AMERICA

Contents

Acknowledgments

For kindnesses granted without question and truths shared with ease
(any errors are all mine), I would like to thank, in Africa,
Tony and Betty Archer, Bill and Ruth Woodley, Danny Woodley,
Calvin Cottar, Ian Parker, Carol Bell, Richard Cox, Gillies Turle,
Fiametta Monicelli, Rajni Desai, Ian Cameron, Willie Nocker,
Jane Perlez and Ray Bonner, Peter, Najma, and Zara Beard;
in the States, Sophie Procter, Annette Bard, Stuart Krichevsky,
Peter and Sandy Riva, Terry Hackford, and Debra Goldman.

Jon Bowermaster
Stone Ridge, New York
February 1993

Here I am,
where I ought to be.

— KAREN BLIXEN

ONE

· · · · · · · · · · ·

Once
the wildlife
is gone,
the only
comparable
thrill will be
found in
the middle of
the biggest cities.

— KAREN BLIXEN

The Remittance Chum

Nairobi was a sprawling, bustling town when Peter Beard first saw it, in 1955: dingy and grubby, friendly and flamboyant, an outback town whose smattering of privileged, overdressed tourists, minor film stars, and colonial fakers imitating Hollywood's great white hunters gave it an air of fifties glamour and authenticity. He loved it.

In truth, Nairobi then was hardly more than a loose gathering of neighborhoods. The occasional lion or leopard still wandered down side roads, and people still lived in shacks in the heart of downtown, squeezed between small hotels and businesses run by East Indians. Peering intently out the rear window of a London cab, Beard now reflects on his first impressions of Nairobi. "It was such a small town then," he says with a smile. "It was as if it hadn't changed in fifty years. The Africans would be out collecting locusts and flying ants for the next meal. You'd go down to the bar at the New Stanley at the end of the day and there would be ten to twenty hunters standing around, commiserating about their most recent lousy clients or bragging about the good old days. You knew everyone; everyone knew everyone. It was perfect."

Those days are long gone, however. Today the twelve-mile drive from the New Stanley Hotel's Thorn Tree Café—once Nairobi's physical and psychological heart—to Beard's forested compound on the outskirts of the city is a riot of bigness. We pass a string of skyscrapers followed by rows of cheap, modern townhouses, then acre after acre of mud and cardboard huts. Alongside the road trudge workers six abreast, shouldering bags of fruit and vegetables. Dangling from each hand are plastic milk containers cut in half and filled with kerosene for their cookstoves.

We make a right turn onto Mukoma Road, once Beard's private, mile-long murram driveway. In the distance the Ngong Hills frame the horizon. When Beard moved here, nearly thirty years ago, the red-dirt road was enveloped by thick forest; today it is paved and lined with Bel-Air-like estates, impregnable behind thick bougainvillea laced with barbed wire. Servants in long gray cotton coats and black rubber boots water and trim

Beard with a
bushbaby,
Kenya,
1971

MAP OF KENYA

AND THE UGANDA RAILROAD

Scale of miles

200 MILES

0 20 40 60 80 100 120 140 160 180 200

BOUNDARIES ○○○○○○○○○

RAILROAD ~~~~~~ (for distance

SWAMP

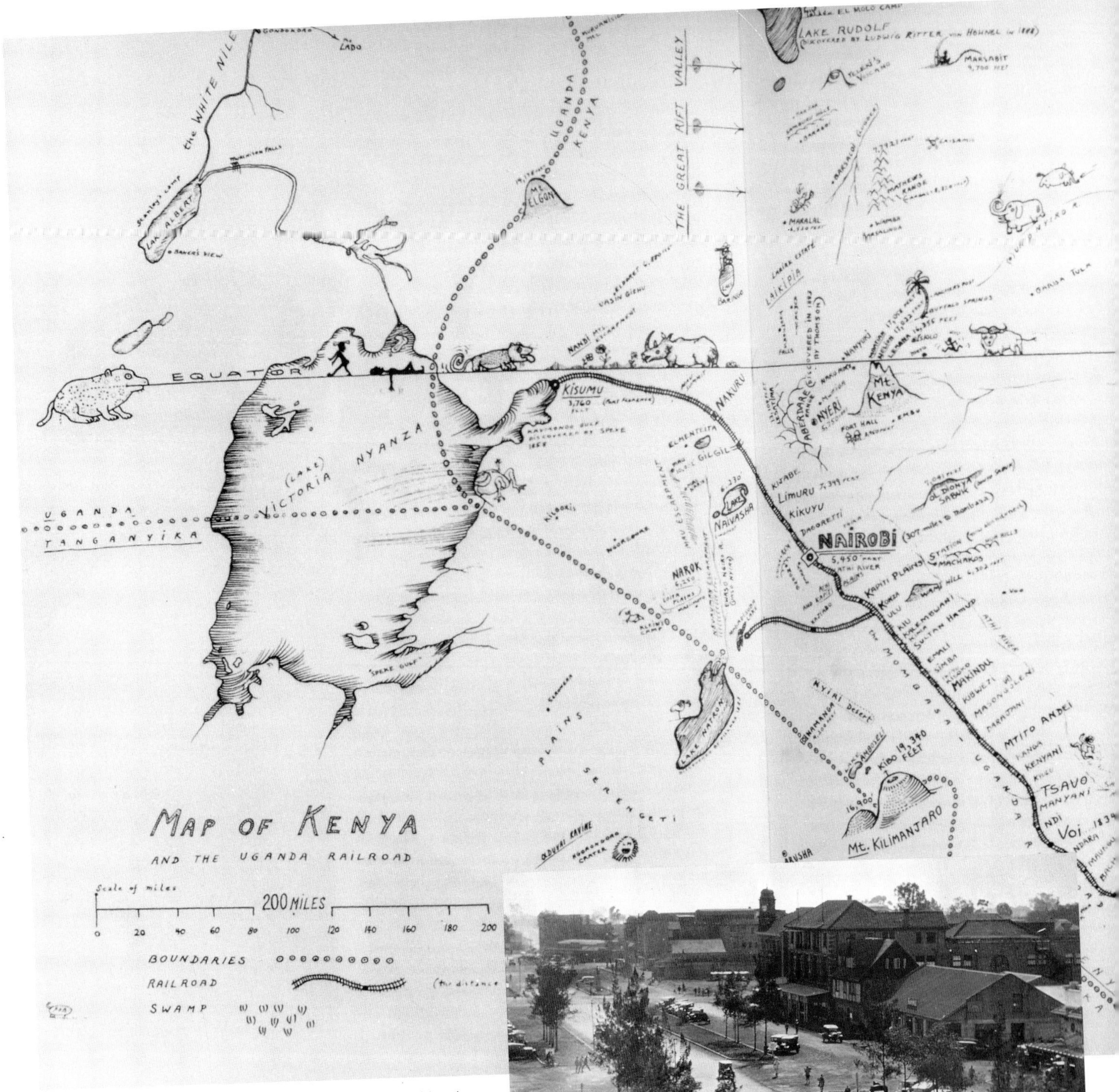

Nairobi,
circa 1940

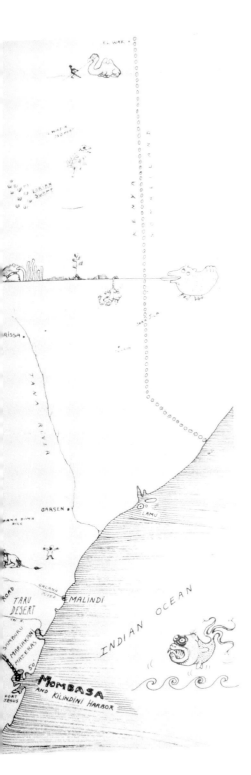

the manicured lawns and guard the electronic gates. Dogs bark. The scent of jasmine, scarlet canna, mimosa, and frangipani rises from gardens that also bear tender English roses, long-stemmed lilies, and fuchsias. Behind the tall hedges are concealed the homes of the self-dubbed "Vanilla Gorillas" (forty-thousand whites live in this city of three and a half million) who call this suburb of Langata home. This neighborhood has become the unofficial residence of much of Kenya's "wildlife gang": clanlike, the country's best-known wildlife experts, safari guides, professional hunters, writers, and filmmakers, as well as one singular photographer, all live within blocks of each other. I have been here just weeks, having come on assignment to try and grasp an understanding of this "singular photographer" and how this place has shaped his life and work. I've spent days studying the more than half a million images he has taken across Africa, acquainting myself with both the intimate and wild pictures of trumpeting elephants and charging lions and the bulging stock of fashion photos of sleek, beautiful women placed against backdrops of pure Africana. I've looked at contact sheet after contact sheet of his most provocative work—the aerials taken from a single-engine plane in the early 1970s that document the writhing deaths of tens of thousands of starving elephants and rhinoceroses. I've seen pictures of Beard in the wild with a variety of faces, including many of the world's most famous and others that I assume are known only to those familiar with the African bush. I've come to Kenya to match his anecdotes with those pictures and to prod him to relive some of his adventures. I'm particularly curious to see firsthand how Kenya—long known as the cornerstone of democracy in Africa, the country that once boasted the best game parks and wildlife scene in the world—has evolved over these past thirty years. I've also come to see how Beard himself has evolved lockstep with the place that has been called his Walden.

Where Mukoma Road dead-ends, a single dirt track leads through a ten-foot-tall fence of green chain link. The fence, a recent addition aimed at keeping wild animals in and human night crawlers out, surrounds Beard's expansive acreage of still-thick forest and acacia trees. A mile inside the gate sits the tent encampment where Beard has resided off and on since 1962. A staff of ten keeps the place running; in all, more than thirty Africans live on the property, including relatives and hangers-on.

Known as Wart Hog Ranch, or simply Hog Ranch (for the grunting packs of wild warthogs that still pay daily visits), the compound sits high atop a ridge overlooking what was once Karen Blixen's six-thousand-acre coffee farm. The view from Beard's campfire is dominated by the Ngong Hills, which Blixen described as "unmovable black waves." Four distinct peaks—Oljoro Onyore, Olorien, Kasmis, and Lamwia—fold together like

3

4

a distant fist; legend holds that the Ngongs were formed from the knuckles of a fallen giant who once plagued the Masai. The hillside forest that Blixen so loved, once covered with acacia thorn and high grass, is now inundated with small farms. The red roofs of stucco-and-cinderblock houses dot the valley and climb the dark green hills.

When Beard first saw the property, it might as well have been in the Pleistocene. To glimpse the Ngongs he had to stand on the roof of his Land Rover; bushbucks, waterbucks, leopards, giraffes, dik-diks, and suni peered out from the enveloping thicket. No more. The nineties Hog Ranch is encircled by a fast-closing suburbia. At night the sounds of shrieking hyraxes and the musical tapping of ground hornbills mix with the pounding of a disco in nearby Ongata Rongai and the barking of pet dogs. An occasional leopard still strolls through the property after dark, but it is marauding gangs of men that the night watchmen (armed with *rungus* [clubs], bows and arrows, and machetes) are hired to keep out.

Beard first came to Africa when he was seventeen; he was looking simply for adventure. The product of a wealthy, patrician New York family, he was desperate to immerse himself in this place that was so different from the streets of Manhattan and the summer houses of Long Island. Like the Europeans who had preceded him at the turn of the century, he wanted to live the wild life, unrestricted by the norms of the high society he was fleeing. In Africa he has lived that life, the kind of life Hemingway fictionalized. He has crisscrossed Kenya dozens of times and walked its borders. For months at a time he has lived in the bush, accompanied only by a solitary native tracker. He has hunted big game, both for food and pleasure and in the name of science. He has followed herds of beasts for days on end, on foot, camera in hand, learning about the animals and about himself. Granted unique permission by park administrators and wardens, he has roamed the savannas and forests of Kenya as few had before him. He has also sought out the surviving colonials and accompanied them on some of the last real safaris to set out across the East African plains.

LEFT

Hog Ranch was named after the wild warthogs who frequent it. Thaka Jr. is the third generation to visit there since Beard arrived in the mid-1960s.

BELOW

Early visitors at Hog Ranch: the monkey, Northi-chongo; Wilhelmina the goat; and Thaka the first

The mess tent at Hog Ranch in 1966.
Minnie Cushing is at the left, Dougie Collins at center.
The buffalo horns that top the tent measure 57¾ inches;
the buffalo was killed by a rhinoceros.

For the past three decades Hog Ranch has served as base camp for Beard's adventures. Around its campfire, in its studio, or atop one of the half dozen treehouses scattered around the property, he has hatched plans for his photography, films, and critically acclaimed books. *The End of the Game,* its first draft written while he was still a student at Yale, stands as classic documentation—in words and pictures—of the fast-evolving relationship between rapacious man and the diminishing wilds. *Eyelids of Morning: The Mingled Destinies of Crocodiles and Men* and *Longing for Darkness: Kamante's Tales from Out of Africa* are books that only Beard could have assembled, both eclectic and prescient, part history, part scrapbook, crammed with existential anxiety and doomsday forecasts. No matter the medium—words, pictures, or films—his take on Africa serves at once as an intriguing introduction for the layman, and a record of just how fast his adopted home has changed since his arrival.

In the course of two lifetimes, Kenya has gone from a state of tribal warfare, through colonialism, past independence, to its current incarnation as a nation ruled by autocracy and paranoia, its wildlife crudely marketed as little more than a series of giant zoos prowled by zebra-striped minibuses. Men whose grandfathers never saw a white man are now entrepreneurs in a booming souvenir economy. Since winning its independence, in 1963, Kenya has wrestled with political freedom only to fail miserably with the whole world watching: Once Africa's proudest model of democracy, today the country is on the verge of civil war. Beard has had a front-row seat for all of this change and has documented not only the thrill of the wilds but also the backslide of a once-hopeful place. Simultaneously, he has been changed, too, affected more than even he may understand by the devolution he has witnessed.

He spends at least half of each year at Hog Ranch, which he has built up from a single tent in the woods to a sprawling compound. The estate includes an all-cedar kitchen, a four-walled studio, a mess tent, a master tent, several guest tents, and a bathtub cloaked by blue canvas. All but the studio are open to the environment, with the result that virtually everything is covered by a patina of rich African dust, in a color that Blixen described as that of "broken pottery." Nothing escapes the ruddy silt, from tables and chairs to the elephant skulls, giraffe femurs, and crocodile armor Beard has collected over the years he has spent traversing the bush. In the studio, a valuable collection of African history books sits under a thick layer of dust, as do framed copies of three covers of *Life* bearing his photographs. Everywhere are piles of sun-bleached fashion magazines, many containing his pictures of women in the wild. In the kitchen hang covers of *Time* and *Newsweek* featuring the gleaming smile of his second wife, Cheryl Tiegs;

9

propped on the floor in the mess tent are signed posters by his friends Francis Bacon, Andy Warhol, and Richard Lindner.

Hog Ranch has served as a Nairobi home-away-from-home to an international cast of actors, models, wildlife experts, retired hunters, writers, wardens and rangers, filmmakers, government officials, and artists, as well as denizens of thc West's most famous families (Kennedys, Du Ponts, Mellons, Rockefellers). All have slept beneath these thatched roofs, hosted by a most congenial Beard. "Well, I'll be a blue-nosed gopher, it's good to see you" is his standard welcome to friends old and new. "Stay for dinner, stay the night, stay as long as you like." To the merry-go-round of guests he is a combination soothsayer, prophet, and party animal. These days he is glad for people to come to him; that way he rarely has to leave the comfort of his leather-backed chairs, the company of the three daily Nairobi papers, his ever-present diary, and the campfire from which he has views of Blixen's farmland and the grave of her fabled lover, Denys Finch Hatton.

The wide cross section of humankind that has graced Hog Ranch is a testament to Beard's one-of-a-kind charisma. When he visits New York City, where he was born, within hours of his arrival he is surrounded by leggy models, each hoping to have her picture taken by "the famous Peter Beard." When he returns to Nairobi, it is the Masai elders who seek him out, coming up from the hills to sit around his campfire, drink small glasses of vodka and orange juice, and listen intently to his rusty Swahili.

Trying to define Beard is difficult. After spending several months touring Kenya in his company, I came away convinced that he was equal parts young Hemingway, turn-of-the-century photographer Edward Curtis, egotistical dilettante, and (as *Newsweek* once described him) "Tarzan with a brain." He is possessed of the kind of looks that stop conversations when he enters the room, and yet he is made up of odd-sized parts, with big hands, big feet, big nose, and big ears. His fingers are almost always stained with India ink—and often his toes as well. Hardly a slave to fashion, he can manage handsomely by donning essentially the same clothes for weeks. His daily uniform in Africa is a V-neck sweater, *kikoi,* or loincloth, and Afghan sandals.

But everyone sees Beard differently. One friend calls him "an American born into wealth and privilege, a charter member of the jet set, [who] could easily pass as a romantic figure right out of Solomon's mines. He has the looks, the bearing, and the natural assurance and flamboyance of the Hollywoodized 'great white hunter.'" Next-door neighbor and photographer/biologist Iain Douglas-Hamilton insists he is a "scavenger"; Kenyan Dr. Harvey Croze dismisses him as a lousy ecologist. Over the

Beard at work on his diary, 1983

decades he has been diversely labeled a naturalist, fashion photographer, prophet of doom, stoic, diarist, garbage collector, felon, bum, racist, anthropologist, social chameleon, raconteur, celebrity, schizophrenic, court jester, despiser of mankind, and eighties existentialist. All and more are true, to varying degrees.

Nothing irks Beard more than being dubbed a "jet-set socialite." Yet he's done little to evade the tag. Since he was old enough to drive, he has courted, been linked with, and even been married to some of the world's most famous models, actresses, daughters (and wives) of billionaires, *Playboy* centerfolds, and royalty. Most people recognize his name for marrying America's sweetheart Cheryl Tiegs, and many of his friends are household names. One day at his stateside house in Montauk, during the course of a couple hours he fielded phone calls from Lee Radziwill's biographer (Jackie O's sister was a longtime sweetheart), Terry Southern (with whom he wrote a screenplay), and Lauren Hutton (one of Hog Ranch's most frequent visitors).

His good friend and reluctant Hog Ranch manager Gillies Turle calls Beard an "obsessive binger." I know what he's talking about, as I've seen it in action. It is a curious state of being that overtakes Beard whether he's chasing a rhino through the bush or at a party in New York. Each has been known to absorb him completely for days on end; just as it was once typical for him to disappear into the bush for days with his camera, without telling anyone of his plan, the same thing happens when he hits the jungle of Manhattan. He has been known to disappear there for days, leaving clues—like his coat, diary, glasses, wallet, shoes—behind. This obsessiveness and passion for the chase carry over into his relationships with friends—men and women alike. He can make you feel favored by his attentiveness or slay you with withering criticism if he disagrees with your opinion. He is a frantic believer in the primacy of experience over the structured recording of it, in the manic integrity of the lived moment. A proud and confessed "remittance chum," a major portion of his annual income is from a pair of family trusts. Everyone who has crossed his path either loves him or is irritated by him, and often both simultaneously. People are drawn to him like moths to a flame. "People enjoy watching him live," wrote critic Larry Shames.

He is complex, smart, gregarious, and soft-hearted; a weaver of tall tales, who is occasionally rude and often class-conscious, a man who truly cares about other people and the world but doesn't want you to know it. He can hold forth day-long around the Hog Ranch campfire and sweep people up with him, attempting to coerce them verbally to his way of thinking, whether the subject is wildlife management, population dynamics, presidential politics, the NFL, or movies. His renowned intensity and self-absorption burn out all but the most diligent listeners. Najma, his third and current wife, describes him as peripatetic, though much less so now that he has passed the fifty-year mark. One particularly calming influence the past few years has been his daughter, Zara, whom he calls "my little loin fruit."

When asked, Beard tells people he is a "diarist," though every white Kenyan knows his reputation and his photographs, which are some of the last, best records of what Africa used to be. Critic Owen Edwards claims Beard's pictures are "photographic art at its most transfiguring"; Francis Bacon called his unique daily diaries "inestimable records of our time." His passion is his work, and he is frustrated by the knowledge that the messages in his books and photographs have been often overlooked. He admits candidly that his best photographic opportunities may be behind him; his closest friends believe that since recording the massive die-off of much of Kenya's wildlife his fascination with the place has died, too. Yet once back in the bush, away from the distractions and temptations of Nairobi or New York, his affinity for the bush life returns, his animal-like instincts are renewed. If there is a sadness to his days now, it is because such forays into the wilds are fewer and fewer.

Although Africa, Kenya, her wildlife, and Beard himself have all witnessed great changes since 1955, Beard's obsessive relationship with his adopted home has remained constant. When he is at Hog Ranch he can be found each morning, feet near the fire in front of the mess tent, reading the local newspapers and scribbling comments in the margins, or working on his diary spread out on a wooden table. Breakfast, prepared and served by Kamau, who has worked at Hog Ranch for eighteen years, is always the same: boiled eggs and toast heavily doused with Lea & Perrins and salt and mixed in a glass mug, chased by a beer stein of *"maji, beridi"* (milk, cold).

On those mornings in front of the fire it seems to Beard like a long time ago, those days in his twenties when he would disappear for months into Africa's wildest landscapes, chasing bongos and lions and elephants, accompanied only by his Leica and a native tracker. Since then he has watched a tornado of events refashion his paradise, but one cool, sunny morning in front of the fire—where we are to spend many hours over several months—Beard backhandedly admits that his initial hopes of Africa have been fulfilled. Handing me pages from a children's book he is writing (*Zara's Tales from Hog Ranch*), he points to a heavily underlined passage: "I came to Africa because I wanted to break free, to escape, to set sail. I came for fun, to fulfill my dreams, to learn something new from something old." His admission comes via the broad smile that accompanies his reminiscing.

TWO

Animals Were All...

It is early on a winter morning, which in Nairobi (elevation over five thousand feet) means it is cool and cloudy. By midday the sun will have burned off the dampness and the temperature risen to seventy. Mornings are the most peaceful time of day at Hog Ranch.. The disco has quieted and the dogs have lost their yap. Turacos call, hyraxes bark and grind, and the air is heavy with small birds—bronze mannikins, blue-capped cordon bleus, firefinches, robin chats, yellow-rumped seedeaters, black cuckoos, and paradise flycatchers dart back and forth over the small meadow that overlooks the Ngongs.

Breakfast has been cleared, and Beard is concentrating on the *Kenya Times,* the daily paper controlled by the country's dictatorial government. He moans and sighs and guffaws as he reads, marking the margins with exclamation points and underlining whole paragraphs he finds most titillating or truthful. Tony Archer, one of Kenya's best-known hunters, guides, and naturalists, and a Langata neighbor, has told me Beard's fixation with the local newspapers is a kind of self-congratulation. "He reads them for stories about environmental degradation and corruption and the like, as a way of vindication, as a way to say 'I told you so.'"

Immersing himself in the papers is also Beard's none-too-subtle way of avoiding my questions. Today's is why he first came to Africa. While outspoken on virtually any subject, when it comes to himself and his own motivations he is unusually circumspect. While he reads he wrestles with how to respond, or ignore, my query.

I know he first visited Africa in 1955, before anyone in his immediate family (his parents Anson and Rosanne and his brothers Anson, Jr., and Sam), though his cousin Jerome once filmed an Academy Award–winning documentary on Albert Schweitzer in the Congo. "Everything I knew about the place came from books," he finally offers. As a boy he had filled his rooms at home and at college with antlers, horns, and the stuffed heads of various animals. "I thought of Africa as a place where there was still plenty of room, where you could actually live life rather than have your

Beard with
Tuxedo Lake bullfrog,
circa 1950

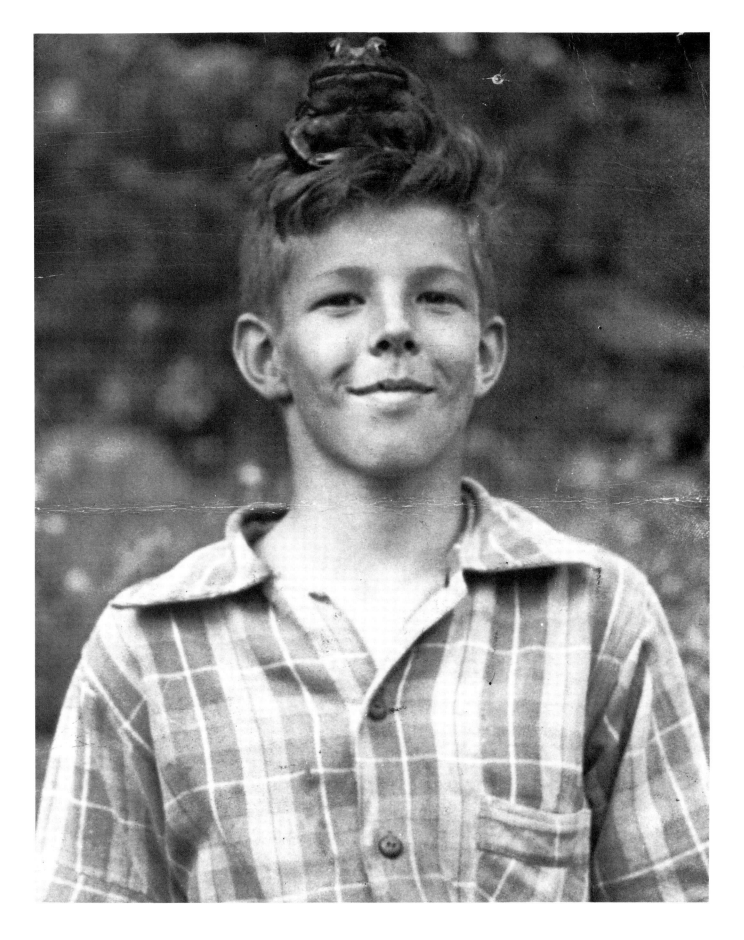

Beard and
Quentin Keynes,
with driver,
1955

life run by a world where you wake up in the morning to a traffic jam, rush to catch a bus, struggle to get to the office . . ."

On a 1954 trip to England with his family, sixteen-year-old Beard read Karen Blixen's *Out of Africa,* which she wrote under the name Isak Dinesen. He credits this singular book with triggering his lifelong obsession with both the authoress and the place she loved. With what he describes as "an incredible amount of luck and a lot of pushiness" he eventually met Blixen, at her home in Denmark. To this day he speaks of her reverentially. "*Out of Africa* was the first meaningful book I'd read and clearly the best," he once wrote. "All the dark mysteries of nature finally found a voice in one of the few outsiders who had the intelligence to go to Africa to listen rather than to tell. She was lucky, of course, she made her luck, to be in one of the greatest places on earth and at possibly the greatest time."

He traveled to Africa for the first time in 1955, accompanied by Quentin Keynes, grandson of Charles Darwin. The two saw Madagascar and South Africa and the grand parks at Umfolozi and Hluhluwe, and made short forays into Tanzania and Kenya.

In 1957 he visited North Africa and in 1960 returned to Kenya for good, more or less. He was between his junior and senior years at Yale. Traveling with a young Frenchman from Madagascar, Rick Fraise, he made the venerable New Stanley Hotel his home away from home. The hotel's Thorn Tree Café was the staging ground for many of Kenya's most famous safaris. Beard was enchanted by the crowd it attracted and the adventure, danger, and romance of the wild they spoke about. "I desperately wanted that wilderness experience," he wrote in his journal.

He was similarly intrigued by the Kenyan version of colonialism that was just then being dismantled. He readily admits he would have preferred to have been born fifty years earlier and to have participated in the colonization of Kenya. In 1980 he told a reporter: "There was a chance, from about the turn of the century to the late 1950s, that East Africa might have been the finest place in history inhabited by humans. [It was] peopled by the most adventuresome, highly educated, eccentric, humorous, really quite daring people, like Karen Blixen, her brother, Thomas Dinesen, Bror Blixen, her friends Ewart Grogan, Philip Percival, Denys Finch Hatton, Lord Delamere, Johnny Boyes, Pop Binks, Ingrid Lindstrom, Rose Cartwright, Charles Bulpett, and many more. All of those early people got along with the Africans and got along with them in the wildest and most isolated, daring circumstances, in exhilarating harmony.

"You would have a mixture of pure, raw authentic tribesmen and these totally genuine and extraordinary pioneers, all making an effort to celebrate their fortune in simply *being* there, the enormous *pleasure* and *privilege* of living in the right place in this vast, open wilderness, a wilderness that was much bigger than anybody now can realize, much more immense and more paradise-like than we can ever know."

It was that Kenya—the Kenya of Isak Dinesen's autobiographical drama—that Beard fell in love with and that drew him to Africa.

. . . .

Peter Hill Beard was born in New York City on January 22, 1938, the middle son of Anson McCook Beard and Rosanne Hoat. His father's family was from Minnesota, where his great-grandfather J. J. Hill had founded the Great Northern Railroad. When Beard's paternal grandfather died his estate was worth $53 million. Growing up, Beard eagerly studied the Daumiers and Corots on the walls of his family's nine-room, East Eighty-first Street apartment.

From 1938 to 1946 the family lived at Maxwell Field Air Force Base in Alabama where his father served in the Army Air Corps; back in New York after the war Peter was enrolled at Buckley, the prep school his father had attended. From an early age Beard was enamored of animals, the outdoors, the wild life. He remembers seeing Gargantua, the famous gorilla in the Ringling Brothers Barnum & Bailey Circus, when he was six. A year later he visited New York's Natural History Museum for the first time, and there he stood for hours in the African Hall, in the dark, studying the roaring, charging herd of stuffed elephants. "Maybe that's why I came to Africa," he writes in *Zara's Tales,* "or maybe it was the screen in my nursery that had painted giraffes, palm trees, and jumping monkeys. Or maybe it was the Walt Disney movie frames on the wall, of Bambi and Dumbo."

Summers were spent in Islip, Long Island, where, according to a nanny, Mrs. Beard gave instructions that the boys were not to be allowed out in the morning until after they had each entered an account of the previous day's activities in their diaries. (Beard remembers her "nagging" at him to write.) In his room a hand-painted plaster-cast rattlesnake curled up in leaves in a wastepaper basket. An aquarium held at various times salamanders, newts, garter snakes, turtles, tortoises, snails, squirrels, chipmunks, raccoons, and possums, all to the chagrin of his mother, who regularly demanded that he keep his creatures out of the house. "But the animals were all that interested me," he writes. Those early fascinations with wildlife were accompanied by an intense desire to get away, to see places museums could only hint at.

Rosanne Beard and her sons— Peter (at left), Anson (standing), and Sam— circa 1943

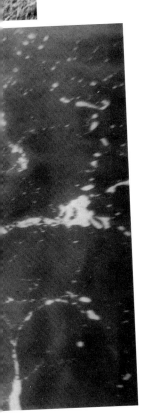

He dutifully continued to follow in his father's academic footsteps, attending Pomfret School in Connecticut from 1950 to 1954 (where he spent his clothing allowance on art books), then Felsted College in Essex, England, and finally Yale, where he enrolled as a premed student. (His mother's desire was to have one son a lawyer, another in government, and the third a doctor. She eventually got two out of three of her wishes.) Soon after enrolling, Beard switched his major to art history, studying under Josef Albers and Richard Lindner. "That was a little unusual," he confesses. "In those days you just didn't *major* in art, at least nobody else did."

He had discovered photography ten years before Yale and once in New Haven quickly replaced physics and economics courses with painting classes and the darkroom. "Photography had become a way of life, a way to preserve and to remember the passing, changing, fast-fading, favorite things," he says.

The first photograph Beard remembers taking was a picture of a governess, a cook, and a maid standing in a driveway on Long Island in 1950. The maid leans against a pram left by the nurse. She is squinting into the sun. The cook wrestles to control a Labrador retriever half out of the picture. Beard was twelve and just happened to be passing by the scene, his Voigtlander Bessa I in his hand. He remembers the picture as the first on the roll, "and probably the finest photograph I have ever taken, fresh, straightforward, genuine and real."

His favorite photographic subjects were bullfrogs, woodcocks, ruffed grouse, snakes, moist neon-orange salamanders with chartreuse spots, freshly laid frog eggs, tadpoles, polliwogs, ducks, deer, and his dog Charcoal. He began to live for the arrival of the yellow Kodak envelopes full of new pictures. Even back then he welcomed the accidents—the bad exposures, high-speed flukes, and out-of-focus images—that ever since have served as the cornerstones of his evocative photographic collages and one-of-a-kind diaries. It wasn't until he found Africa that his passions and his artistry combined to propel him into a life unmatched in its spontaneity, creativity, success, and disillusionment.

21

Photographs and painting from Beard's childhood

THREE

. . . .

... country so lovely, as if the contemplation of it could in
itself be enough to make you happy all your life.

— KAREN BLIXEN

Jolly Pioneers of Progress

The colonials often shared that strange sensation common to
exiled Englishmen of being "out of bounds." Many
of them had money. Many were remittance men who had been paid off
by their families and sent away in disgrace. Once their spirits
and sense of status had been restored by this feudal paradise,
the temptation to behave badly was irresistible, and both men and
women often succumbed to "the three A's"
—altitude, alcohol and adultery.

— JAMES FOX, *White Mischief*

To understand the magnetic pull the dark continent exerted on Beard, to get a sense of the magic drumbeat that lured him to Kenya, you must have some understanding of the country's history. Particularly important is the arrival of the British colonists at the turn of the twentieth century, whom Conrad called "jolly pioneers of progress."

What remains of Kenya's colonial past introduces itself to me on a crisp May night at a masked ball in the heart of the suburb of Karen (named in the 1940s for the author whose coffee farm once dominated the valley). "It will be just like the good old days," jokes Beard as we scribble India ink on one-dollar masks picked up at a downtown discount store.

On the spacious back lawn of the Seex House—No. 1 Mbagathi Ridge, across the street from the Blixen homestead—the glittery Harambee (Unity) party is being held to raise money for the twelve-year-old son of one of the household staff, who needs medical help for a heart defect. The host is a second-generation white Kenyan who made his money on restaurants in Nairobi and Mombasa (particularly the glitzy Carnivore restaurant/disco on the outskirts of Kenya's capital city). The stone and wood mansion had been built by his father in the 1920s, adjacent to Denys Finch Hatton's runway.

Peter Beard
with Karen Blixen
in Rungstedlund,
Denmark,
July 1962

23

Much of this pleasant winter night is spent warming hands around a sizable bonfire. Giant plywood masks decorate the lawn; white tents cover fifty elegantly set tables. A disc jockey pumps out hits, followed by a jazz band from Zaire. Venison, shrimp, peapods, and Thai chicken highlight the buffet. Young and old dance beneath a rotating disco ball and roam between the linen-draped tables and fully stocked bar. A kidney-shaped pool and the estate's massive trees—figs, fevers, and euphorbias—are spotlit. The tuxedoed and elaborately masked crowd is equal parts young Kenyan cowboys and stooped old men. Beard knows a smattering from each generation.

The masked ball
in Karen,
1991

All eyes had followed Beard when we strolled in, sans tuxedos. He doesn't mingle with this crowd much anymore, preferring the constantly revolving scene around the Hog Ranch campfire. After a quick survey he makes the rounds, gin and tonic in hand. He regales the younger men with tall tales from the old days, the telling reminding them that he's been here a long time. To reinforce this message he tosses out unsubtle declarations, like "I passed through South Africa in 1955 . . . " or "I was in Isiolo before you were born."

With equal bravado he chats up the old boys, their white hair slicked back, beaks red from years in the bush and the bars, bodies bent from tropical diseases, animal scarrings, and accidental shootings. They trade reminiscences and current gossip, recall cherished drunken nights in the bush and favored "boys" (the incredibly outdated terminology many white Kenyans still use for the black men who worked by their side, as aides-de-camp or household help), and the time Beard held a puff adder from behind. "They are hard to hold safely, even from the back of the head, because their jaws literally unhinge," Beard says, as several old coots nod with understanding. "If you're not careful they'll twist their heads around and deliver the *fait accompli!*"

Beard has witnessed incredible change in Kenya, and faster, more turbulent times than have occurred almost anywhere on the planet. When he first visited, the Mau Mau uprising—black rebels taking to the hills to fight white colonials—was ongoing. Though the uprising was crushed soon after, the country was never to be the same. Across the continent 1960 was known as "the Year of Africa." In a matter of months seventeen African colonies became independent; on a single day, September 20, sixteen African nations were admitted to the UN. Independence came officially to Kenya in 1963 and white Kenyans became just another tribe. The romanticized days of European rule were gone; the real world, bringing along its package of progress and woe, had caught up with Beard's paradise. Recording its evolution (or devolution) would become his passion.

Jomo Kenyatta,
center,
Scotland Mission Church,
Kikuyu,
1968

It is easy to see why Kenya attracted the early white pioneers. Bigger than France, a tad smaller than Texas, it was at the turn of the century one of the most majestic and captivating places on earth. Straddling the equator, its temperatures are moderated by altitude. Thus, the coast was tropical, the deserts hot, and much of the game country comfortable. The Central Highlands around mile-high Nairobi were blessed with an eternally spring-like climate. Scenery ran the gamut from volcanic lakes to mountain rain forests, from the soft greens of the Rift Valley to snow-capped Mount Kenya (where the air was exceptionally clear and pure and was said to produce "euphoria" in Europeans, who therefore could not be held accountable for their behavior).

When the Europeans arrived coffee, maize, and sisal grew very profitably and there was excellent pastureland for stock. Game was everywhere: Millions of flamingos nested in the mountain lakes; buffalo, eland, and rhinoceros roamed the hills; elephants flourished in both the dry bush country and the rain forest; giraffes grazed the spreading thorn trees; monkeys chattered in the forest; and the savannahs were home to herds of zebra, wildebeest, and gazelle, who in turn fed their feline predators. Nowhere on earth did life offer such a spectacle of vigor, beauty, harmony, and, above all, scale. It evoked a feeling of religious awe, a sense of gratitude in many of those who beheld it for the first time. Carl Jung, as quoted by Blixen's biographer Judith Thurman, wrote of the Athi Plain, "This was the stillness of the eternal beginning, the world as it had always been."

Caucasians were not completely foreign to Kenya. Arabs and Persians congregated along its coast in the seventh and eighth centuries, the Chinese came in the fifteenth century, and the Portuguese arrived at the beginning of the sixteenth. When the European powers met in Berlin in 1885 to carve up much of Africa among themselves, it was agreed that the British "sphere of influence" would include Kenya, while Germany would take Tanganyika (now Tanzania) to the south. Modeled after the Hudson's Bay Company and the British East India Company, the Imperial British East Africa Company received a royal charter, replete with its own flag, postage stamps, capital city, army, and money. The colonial administration urged settlers to come to Kenya, and they did by the thousands, attracted by the promise of virtually free land, plentiful, cheap labor, and large profits. Most settled in Kenya's fertile Central Highlands, often displacing Africans as they did so. Simultaneously, treaties with the Masai opened up vast quantities of their once-exclusive lands to the Kikuyu and other tribes.

Nairobi came into being in 1899, initially as just a settlement created by the British at Mile 327 of the East African railroad line, which was then being systematically forged from the coast to the Ugandan border. The railroad's construction was modern man's first real war against nature in Kenya; as mile after mile of track was laid, dozens of species—from elephants to secretary birds—were chased from their homes. In some instances the beasts did not go peacefully. Man-eating lions haunted the railway's construction camps, stealing in after dark and dragging men from their tents. Even armed guards could not deter the lions from their mission, and dozens of workers were killed.

The site that became Nairobi was originally a supply depot, switching yard, and campground for the thousands of Indian laborers employed by the British to help build the railroad. Bleak and swampy, it was simply the spot where operations came to a halt while the engineers figured out their next move, namely, getting the line up the steep slopes that lay ahead. The town's name came from the Masai term for the valley, *Ewaso Nairobi,* Stream of Cold Water.

By 1907 Nairobi was firmly established and had become the capital of British East Africa. Two years later, when Teddy Roosevelt led his famed hunting expedition from the Norfolk Hotel with more than a hundred porters, the city was forever established as the safari capital of the continent. It became the base for Kenya's famous hunter/wanderers: Ewart "Cape-to-Cairo" Grogan, one of Karen Blixen's best friends, whose fame and nickname came from his having walked the length of the continent; J. H.

26

The District Commissioner's office, shortly after completion, Nairobi, 1913

Prisoners being marched down Government Road in Nairobi, 1916

Patterson, the benevolent pioneer who oversaw construction of the railroad to Uganda; R. J. Cogninghome and Leslie Tarleton, Roosevelt's handpicked expedition leaders; and legendary hunters, including J. A. Hunter, Pat Ayre, Allan Black, Tiger Marriott, Hoey Judd, and, perhaps the most famous of them all, Philip Percival, Bror Blixen's safari company partner.

Throughout the twentieth century the well-to-do with little to do made Kenya their African playground, and the safari mystique was born. Idealized in literature and film, the glamorous figure of the white hunter— "fearless, independent, cultivated, yet cynical, hard-drinking, irresistible to women," is how Kenya's literary historian Elspeth Huxley described the stereotype—became an icon of modern African mythology. "Kenya" became synonymous with "safari" (the word's Arabic root means "to journey or travel").

Increasing numbers of Europeans were attracted by this growing mystique: undercapitalized farmers, aristocrats, bourgeois wanderers, writers, con men, carpetbaggers, missionaries, amusement seekers weary of or cast out from other climes or other countries, misfits, and neurasthenics. Most were of great breeding and charm, such as bounders like Josslyn Hay of *White Mischief* fame, who was described by associates as "a first class fellow, like a lot of those who never had anything to do." "Clever, always had a brain, always an answer." "Attractive chap." Many of the new

27

The King's
African Rifles on
Victoria Street,
1907

Ewart S. Grogan
1874 — 196??

to. My good friend Peter Beard.

J. A. Hunter
Hunters Lodge.
Kenya.

June 23. 1960. and 12-12—61
" The end of the Game. "

Tania Blixen.
Rungstedlund

Philip H Percival.
Sept 1905 - Dec. 31. 1961 †

A Beard diary page from June 1960 signed by early pioneers Ewart "Cape-to-Cairo" Grogan,
J. A. Hunter, Karen ("Tania") Blixen, and Philip Percival

Philip Percival
and Peter Beard at
the Nguruman
escarpment camp,
1971

arrivals had money to spare and no great interest in making a profit, earning themselves the disparaging description of "veranda farmers."

Such were the role models and lifestyles admired by the modern-day remittance chum and neocolonial, Beard. He was perfect for Kenya: handsome, educated, articulate, monied, carefree. He, too, felt somewhat chased out of his homeland by a passion to explore and run wild—in Karen Blixen's words, to "set sail." Bringing with him vast energy and little discipline, keen intelligence and scattered thinking, huge generosity and egregious egocentricity—eccentric to the very marrow—Beard arrived at the best or worst possible moment. The game was already in full retreat along with a way of life. A nation of hunters for thousands of years was becoming a nation of farmers and city dwellers. As the human population swelled, animals were already in reserves; the wilderness was shrinking.

When we leave the masked ball near dawn, Beard insists on a driving tour of the suburb of Karen. From the front seat he points out historical points of interest: Karen Blixen's pond, her driveway, Ndege Road, which was Finch Hatton's runway, the corner of Ngong Road where Josslyn Hay was found dead in his car, the lights on, the motor running. Each bend in the road holds a rich history, and Beard relishes his role as tour guide.

After just a few hours of sleep, we drive back to the same neighborhood for an early-morning visit to Karen Blixen's house, Mbogani (House in the Woods). Standing in the curved, stone driveway, looking at the small but elegant seventy-seven-year-old dwelling, Beard turns quiet, reverential. "Can you imagine the atmosphere of the old Africa?" he asks. "Can you imagine the safaris that used to come and go out of these doors?"

Built of stone and cedar in 1914, the house has low ceilings and narrow halls. Three small bedrooms wrap around the library, dining room, and study. The bathroom (reached from the outside through a small door, so staff could carry in bathwater) has a tin tub and compost toilet. The kitchen is in a separate building. Beard leads from room to room, pointing out Karen's desk and typewriter, an original map of the six-thousand-acre farm, Finch Hatton's books on the library shelf, the mirror in the bedroom ("That was her mirror," he whispers, "she must have looked in it thousands of times"). He studies the tall, deep, stone fireplace and explains that this is where Karen entertained Finch Hatton with stories long into the night.

Seated on a window seat with four-year-old Zara, Beard looks out at the Ngong Hills and, speaking simply, explains that "Karen Blixen, who was a very good friend, used to sit here for hours and watch the sunset and listen to the lions roar." (He does not tell her of Karen's suffering from waves of deep depression, loneliness, and syphilis.)

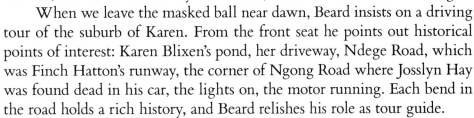

Peter Beard
in the Aberdares,
circa 1966

29

30

On the way back to Hog Ranch we pass the estate of Sid Downey, founder of Kenya's premier safari company, Ker & Downey. Beard tells me that Downey tried on numerous occasions to meet Karen Blixen, as had many white Kenyans. She refused most who asked. Beard, on the other hand, spent many days in her company.

Blixen left Kenya in July 1931, after seventeen years, and sailed home to Denmark. Over a million dollars of her family's money had been lost on her dream. Her marriage was over, her coffee plantation auctioned. Her memoirs of those years became *Out of Africa,* published in 1938 (the year Beard was born).

Beard's meeting Blixen is a classic example of his persistence, audaciousness, and luck—all traits Blixen admired and possessed herself. On his way to Kenya in December 1961 to arrange a safari for himself and college friend Bill Du Pont, Beard stopped in Denmark, hoping to meet the by-then octogenarian authoress. "It is interesting to speculate on why she agreed to meet me," he says this day, seated at the millstone behind Mbogani, "because she hated talking to anyone about Africa. She refused to meet Bill Holden and many others."

At the time, Blixen was dying of a variety of illnesses, living primarily on glasses of fruit and vegetable juice, ampules of gelle royale, oysters, and dry biscuits. Her emaciated, eighty-five-pound body was wracked by stomach problems. According to biographer Judith Thurman, "The flesh of her face hung from her bones, her skin bruised at the touch. Advanced syphilis of the spine made it difficult for her to stand."

"I had written her before about my first visits to Kenya and gotten a very poetic and thoughtful letter back," remembers Beard, "but she didn't say come visit me or anything. I was taking the *Bremen* to Southhampton on my way to Africa and sent her a radio telegram from the boat, asking if I could stop in for a visit. I got no reply."

Not easily discouraged, he boarded a plane for Copenhagen. Seated next to him was a Dane who happened to be a friend of Blixen's favorite niece, Bitter. "He gave me her name and number and suggested I stay at the Angleterre." When Beard arrived at the exclusive hotel, there were no rooms available. Disappointed, he turned to leave, but as he neared the door he was stopped by the hotel's manager, who asked him, "What did you say your name was?"

"Peter Beard," the young American responded, and the manager told him he had a message for him. "It was a note from Karen Blixen. She had guessed that I would go to the Angleterre and had arranged a room for me. It was incredibly heavy." She invited him to come to her home, called Rungstedlund, later that day.

"I arrived, and her longtime assistant, Clara Svendsen, answered the door," remembers Beard. "'Oh, I'll just go get the baroness now,' she said and rushed upstairs, leaving me in the hallway with a pile of books and diaries under my arms. I turned around and around in the tiny hall, exploring a little office full of Masai spears and paraphernalia. I was alone for five or six minutes before I felt a haunting feeling, like I was being watched. Sure enough, Karen Blixen was peering in from behind a crack in the hinge side of the door; she had been observing me for at least five minutes. I could see her little beady eye looking through the crack. I walked around as if it was quite normal and said, 'Oh, Baroness, it's wonderful to see you!'"

Beard stayed in Copenhagen for two weeks, moving in with Bitter and Karen Blixen's brother, Thomas Dinesen. He visited Karen twice more, showed her his initial writings and pictures from Kenya, and photographed her. He never asked why she had allowed him to come. "I was lucky," he says, looking out at the Ngongs. "I did have a clue, though. Clara Svendsen told me she thought it might have been that I looked a little bit like Denys Finch Hatton." Karen Blixen died nine months after Beard met her, on September 6, 1962.

In retrospect, granting the young Beard an audience was not so unusual. According to Judith Thurman, "Her door was open to anyone who wanted to discuss her work seriously. She challenged [young people] in a way they found irresistible; she listened to them in a manner that made them feel extraordinary and unique." Blixen's brother chided her in her later years for "the manner in which she held forth seductively to a circle of boys young enough to be her grandsons." In the months before she received Beard, she had had visits from Aldous Huxley and Timothy Leary.

Meeting Karen Blixen profoundly shaped Beard's take on Kenya. "She was one of the very few people who ever went to Africa who managed to get it down truthfully and meaningfully into a book," he wrote in a letter to a friend. "Hemingway failed in *Green Hills,* almost everybody failed. But she came away with something very close to the greatness of the wilderness where all these traumatic and extraordinary experiences were lived. *Out of Africa* represents the best of what Africa means to me. It is the most profound work that will ever be done in this country, and one of the finest books in the English language. Her writing tells us that nature is the most important thing in our lives, and the closer people and animals are related, the more meaningful, genuine, authentic, relaxing, and life-enhancing it will all be."

Last portrait of
Karen Blixen,
1962

a giraffe is so much a lady, that one refrains from
too remembers her as floating over the plains in
of morning mist or twilight.

Karen Blixen

Dear Mr. Beard,

I am very sorry that my absence on a journey to France and a later illness have prevented me from answering you before.

Very few matters could move me as deeply as your epitaph, or monument, over that Old Africa which was so dear to my heart, - the continent of wisdom, dignity and deep poetry, equally expressed in nature, beast and man.

I think Mr. Hunter's introduction a very fine piece of writing, and your photographs highly impressive. But I do not know what you want me myself to do about your project. I have given my own feelings and convictions expression twenty-five years ago in my book "Out of Africa" and later on in my recent book "Shadows on the Grass", both of which give, I think, much your own views. I feel that it is time for a younger generation to take up the cause. My friend, Count Ahlefeldt, has made me become a life member of an association for the preservation of the African game. He, and the board of it out in Kenya, seem to believe that it is not altogether too late.

My own relation to the world of ancient Africa was indeed a kind of love-affair: love at first sight, and everlasting. I still get letters from my old servants there. Now in your photographs I seem to receive a greeting from the fauna of the country, very dear, noble old friends. I have already got a few native drawings of game, the ones you sent me were fascinating and highly pleasant.

If this letter gives you nothing more, it will at least, I trust, convey to you my profound sympathy with your book.

Believe me, with my kindest greetings,

yours ever

Karen Blixen.

35

As much as Beard admires Blixen, if it were possible for him to be transported back to those days, it's a toss-up as to who he would rather be: her or Denys Finch Hatton. Sitting around the Hog Ranch fire any night, Bloody Bull in hand, he regularly drops the names of the early settlers (Grogan, Patterson, Percival, Black, Binks, et al.), as if he is expecting them to drop by for a cocktail. But the name he most often mentions is Finch Hatton's, whose grave is visible across the valley, high on Lamwia, a slope of the Ngongs. One winter night, when we were together outside the back door of the Shagwong Bar and Grill in Montauk, he paused at the front end of his BMW and laughingly pointed to the license plate. "Maybe that should be DFH," he said. Though we'd had a few beers, I didn't get the sense he was joking.

The similarities between Beard and Finch Hatton are many. Finch Hatton was tall, witty, lean, wry, balding, handsome, aristocratic, with a love of art, music, and poetry that was rare among settlers. To his friends he was a life enhancer who attracted larger-than-life personalities as companions. An individualist, he was often haunted by depression. Finch Hatton had left England to escape the conventional life of his class and because he wanted to explore. Within four weeks of arriving in Kenya he had traveled hundreds of miles, purchased land, formed a partnership, and met the leading personalities of the colony. He was firmly convinced of the country's bright potential for expansion and his future in it.

Finch Hatton was also a writer and a photographer. In January 1928 the *London Times* published a story he'd written: ". . . after taking several still pictures of them under the trees I spent four hours watching animals. I cannot remember having spent a more interesting four hours. During this fortnight we saw roan antelope, buffalo, cheetah, leopard, waterbuck, klipspringers, impala, Grant's and Thompson's gazelles besides immense quantities of the commoner sorts of game. Unfortunately it is a melancholy fact that unless some effective form of legislation is brought in by the Government concerned, this unique state of plenty is doomed to disappear in the very near future." Beard's copy of Errol Trzebinski's biography of Finch Hatton is a riot of underlines, asterisks, and marginalia (*"This is key!!!"* is typical).

Beard is a curious amalgamation of all those he admires, his life formed by a wide variety of influences ranging from early colonialists, professional hunters, and conservationists to a spectrum of modern-day artists and

Denys Finch Hatton,
circa 1924

Photograph by
Denys Finch Hatton,
circa 1922,
of an elephant
shot on control

thinkers. Tony Archer has known Beard for thirty years and says without blinking that his American friend's biggest misgiving is that he wasn't born to this life, that he does not carry a Kenyan passport. Beard laughs when he hears this. "Are you kidding? Into this stinking rot?" But his joking response is a façade. Beard is enthralled still with the romance of early-twentieth-century Kenya and in love with the idea of a life lived in those wilder days.

Before we leave Mbogani, or Karen House, after an hour's visit and pictures around the millstone table, I ask just how much he wishes he'd explored these plains fifty years earlier. He evades the question with this response: "Let's just say it has always been very reassuring to know that Hog Ranch was on the very edge of Karen's property."

38

Aerial view
of Mkomazi-Tsavo,
1975

FOUR

I got in
on the last
months of
everything,
the last gasps
of the great,
old Africa.

— BEARD

Into Africa:
Echoes in the Glasses

Beard's timing was fortuitous. He arrived in Kenya when the nation was entering an era of incredible shakeup, both political and environmental. He was fortunate to meet and befriend the last generation of settlers before they died, including J. A. Hunter, Philip Percival, "Cape-to-Cairo" Grogan, Karen Blixen, and others. He quickly assimilated himself into the group of young white Kenyans—politicians, scientists, entrepreneurs, and hunters—who would emerge as the country's leaders in the years to come.

Beard's early years in Kenya were spent primarily in the bush. He hunted at first for fun, then joined teams of wildlife experts engaged in scientific studies that included culling the then-massive herds of elephants, hippopotamus, buffalo, lions, and zebras. He witnessed firsthand the impact of man's fast-expanding growth on wildlife. While his greatest goal remained adventure, those early years taught him invaluable lessons about man and nature, lessons that would drastically shape his intellect and form his work.

Today, for all his ramblings and eccentricities, it is rare to hear Beard brag about his own bush adventures. Occasionally, in the company of his peers around a campfire late at night, he'll engage in a little one-upmanship, but rarely with those he regards as less experienced. The bottom line is that in his early Kenyan days he saw the last vestige of the real Africa and lived it the way his predecessors had.

The differences between his real experience and his perceived life in Kenya were brought into sharp focus one night at another fancy gathering in Karen. After dinner Beard and I listened to a trio of young men boast about a recent fishing trip in which they had cast over a three-and-a-half-foot crocodile with a barbed hook, snaring it and dragging it back to shore. They were obviously quite taken with their adventure and crowed like the grown boys they were over their shared moment of machismo.

*Zebra skins
at Gilbert Colvile's
Lariak Estate,
1960*

Friends and admirers of Beard's, but younger by at least two decades, they obviously didn't know much about him. Nor, probably, had they ever read his books, though they each proudly told him they owned copies. If they had read his books they most likely wouldn't have been bragging in front of him about their croc catch, since before they were even enrolled in grade school Beard had spent years in the bush hunting every kind of game, in settings and situations they could only dream about.

In 1966, for example, just returned from weeks of hunting crocodiles near the Ethiopian border, Beard was having breakfast alongside Lake Rudolf. His table sat a hundred yards from shore, and his rifle lay at his feet. A gaggle of Turkana kids were splashing around in the shallows when Beard—midway through his eggs and toast—spotted a monstrous crocodile, head very low in the water, following them in the early morning chop. "All I could see was its snout, but I picked up my .270, aimed and squeezed off a careful shot. I was sure I'd missed since there was no flapping of the tail, a guaranteed indication of a brainshot. But the Africans were convinced I'd gotten it, so I went into the water to look around. I dove about twenty times into the soupy gulf before finally touching it. It was a big one, about five feet across; I felt the top of its head and the crease of my silver-tipped bullet. My finger went right into its crinkly cranium . . . and the son of a bitch was just lying there, in an uncertain state of consciousness."

Beard ignored the dazed croc's occasional twitching and wrestled it to the surface by getting underneath it and crawling toward shore. A crowd of a hundred Turkana had gathered to watch the struggle. Once ashore the croc proved a giant at nearly sixteen feet long. In order to preserve the beast's valuable skin, three hundred to four hundred pounds of salt were needed immediately—salt that was six miles away by boat. Beard motored after it, leaving the gathered throng to "guard" the prehistoric creature. When he returned, however, the crocodile was nowhere to be seen. The Turkana were apoplectic as they reported what had happened: The croc had apparently "come alive" and twitched itself back into the water. Beard was forced to go back into the murky depths and lug the brute ashore for a second time, to the delight of the crowd.

The bush experiences of the three young storytelling men at the dinner party seem pale by comparison to Beard's. After their croc experience they retired to a four-star restaurant and spent the night comfortably snug under goosedown duvets at a Mombasa resort. Beard, at the time of his, was sleeping under a tarpaulin rigged in the sand, living off Hellmann's mayonnaise and Ritz crackers. The analogy is not so much an indictment of these young men as it is just one example of how much adventure has changed in the late twentieth century, even in Kenya.

"Monster pebbleworm"
at Lake Rudolf,
1966

· · · · · · · · · · ·

When Beard decided in the early 1960s to become a part-time resident of Nairobi, he took a room at the New Stanley Hotel, where the action was. He would come down in the morning, get a small table at the Thorn Tree, and buy the papers. Before long several tables would be pulled together, and fifteen to twenty people would be drinking coffee, eating, and sharing their most recent escapades. Some of them are still among Beard's best friends in Africa: Tony and Betty Archer, Bill Woodley and his wife, Ruth Hales, John Sutton, Glen Cottar, John Fletcher, Murray Watson, and Mike Prettejohn. From those long brunches he latched on to the best safaris of his life.

In 1961 Ruth Hales worked for the safari company Ker & Downey, which had a kiosk at the hotel. Knowing that Beard was looking for a guide to the bush, she introduced him to Douglas Tatham Collins (known as "Ponsumby"), one of the most colorful hunters in Kenya and a former district commissioner of Somaliland. An incurable romantic and confirmed bachelor, Collins first helped Beard purchase a fourth-hand Land Rover and a cheap 9.3-millimeter gun. Pooling their resources—Beard's bought the Land Rover loaded with food; Collins's, the native trappers, gun bearers, and cook—the two set off for the first of many tours of the Northern Frontier District, or NFD, Kenya's northernmost desert and bush country.

Collins was itching to get back to Somaliland, and the only way to do that was by driving through Kenya's forbidding desert, known as the Greater Shag. Beard was along as hunting partner and to help defray expenses. Each gained something from the other: Collins, an enthusiastic hunting partner; Beard, a remarkable look at what was still incredibly wild country. This was no photo safari, no luxury tented tour, just two guys with guns exploring by following the narrow dirt path that led north from Nairobi.

44

Thorn Tree Café
at the
New Stanley Hotel,
Nairobi,
1961

Beard
recovering from
malaria in the
Nairobi Hospital,
1968

The night before they set out on their first safari, Beard and Collins joined a big group for dinner at the Banda, a small inn outside of Nairobi along Magadi Road. Beard spent much of the night talking with Harold Prowse, an American who came to Kenya as an "in-transit tourist" during the Mau Mau days and never left. A Harvard Business School graduate, Prowse was the first to suggest to the young Beard that "the end of the

game" was approaching. It was a theme—and a phrase—Beard would not forget.

In Collins's company Beard saw virtually every hectare of wild Kenya: from the open plains under Mount Kilimanjaro to Tsavo West and then northward, through Makindu to the desert of the NFD. They spent months away from Nairobi. Along the way Beard sought out the last living remnants of the pioneering days. He interviewed, photographed, and learned from these men whose reputations had been secured in the writings of Blixen and others. He listened intently to their amazing tales from the past and forecasts for the future. He had come to Kenya in many ways a blank slate, and these first journeys became indelibly chalked on his mind.

Beard also met natives in the bush and struck lifelong friendships with experienced trackers and hunters of many tribes, like Mbuno, who then worked with Dougie Collins. The two got on so well that when Collins and Beard split up, Mbuno stayed behind with Beard, with whom he worked, in the bush and at Hog Ranch, until his death in July 1992. Now his son has taken his place.

Every day Beard traveled with Collins brought new encounters with a plethora of beasts, including black rhinos, lions, cheetahs, hippos, buffalo, and massive herds of elephants, reticulated giraffes, gazelles, dik-diks, and warthogs. He suffered through the hot desert life of the NFD, discovered the mystery of the African night, and heard strange legends about snakes that could run as fast as men and elephants with tusks so large that they had to walk backward.

Along the way they hunted for sport and food. In fact, hunting was one of the primary reasons the young Beard was so excited about Kenya; he admired the lives of the great hunters and was anxious to experience something akin to what they had had. He had learned to shoot as a boy in Alabama and Long Island and was an excellent marksman. His first kill in Africa was a hippo at Donya Sabuk. Mbuno handed him a .375, and he took careful aim using a tree as a rest. "It wasn't a hard shot, but it had to be done right, within about two inches of the ear," he recalls. "Up came the head of the cow with its distended eyes. A rifle crack ruptured the silence; a thud and a monstrous sinking. Not a bird or anything stirred. The kill had been too quick for me to know exactly how I felt; it was strangely exciting. The result was two tons of meat, which was carved up for workers on a nearby estate." Following kills were more dangerous and exhilarating. One rainy evening, for example, he shot a leopard with a .375 broken in half and at the last minute tied together with a rope. The leopard jumped five feet in the air and then fell to the ground dead; the rifle shot that killed it knocked Beard to the ground and bloodied his eye.

These were not big-money safaris. When Collins and Beard ran out of food or grew tired of trying to eat zebra (often cooked in a can of sand and gasoline when no wood existed and no thorns burned), they survived on spaghetti, passion fruit, *posho* (white rice), biscuits, and Fig Newtons. One Sunday, hungry and in search of dinner, Beard made a long, hasty shot at an impala, wounding it. In the hot pursuit that followed he tripped in a warthog's hole, breaking his left ankle in two places. "The impala died nearby, and I crawled up to watch these two hungry Turkana boys pulling it apart and gobbling up the kidneys raw. They broke the bones to suck out marrow, the sound of which was beyond description."

Beard and Collins split up after three months, Collins continuing on to Somalia and Beard heading for Laikipia, two hundred miles north of Nairobi, to learn the intricacies of "game control." He took a job on the ranch of Gilbert Colvile, who had begun with eight Boran cows in the 1940s and twenty years later had amassed a herd of ten thousand. Unfortunately, cows and wildlife could not coexist in the same fields because of tick-borne diseases transmitted by the nondomesticated beasts. The only alternative for farmers anxious to squeeze profit from their fenced-in land was to eliminate the competitive game. As well as being challenging hunting, this was to serve as a first, as well as firsthand, introduction for Beard to the effect on wildlife when humans move in.

The work was hard, the stalks long, and the shooting fast—usually from quite a distance. Unlike trophy hunting, in which the target lies in a single vital area of the body, in control work, after the first steady, calculated shot, everything is on the run. To help round up zebras Beard and his bushmates rode horses with jury-rigged saddles. His was a one-eyed steed with a penchant for crashing half-blind through tree limbs. "It was not all amusing," Beard wrote at the time. "My nameless steed would skid and crash into obstacles that sent his head back into mine, resulting in constantly bloodied lips."

The main targets were zebras, buffalo, and cattle-killing lions, and plenty of each were shot. A day's hunting began with a painstaking, tedious stalk until a skittish herd was within range. The shooters made certain that each gun could bring down two or three animals. Back at camp fresh skins were pegged down for salting and dried ones from the previous day were stacked. Dinner was around seven o'clock, and sleep came soon after dark.

It was arduous, dangerous, enlightening work. (Though Beard calls it "work," as in virtually all his nonphotography experiences in the bush he was never paid, per his request.) He remembers one day in particular, running after buffalo full out, carrying heavy guns. "Bryan Coleman, a professional hunter, carried a fourteen-pound .577, which could stop a

47

Record-class leopard in the Mara on the Seria Escarpment, 1969

Cape buffalo,
Masai Mara,
1961

buffalo by sheer impact. I had a slightly disintegrating Husquarua 9.3-millimeter I had bought from an elephant-control officer in the New Stanley's Long Bar. It might seem that running through the narrow, 'wait-a-bit' thorn-pulling tunnels would be the most exhausting part of the ordeal, but it was not. There was an intense exhilaration as we plunged on faster and faster, snapping branches and pulling through vines, soaked with sweat, thinking of nothing but how that bull would look, how long the dogs could hold it at bay, how far apart the horns would be, how big and how mean it would be.

"Ahead of me Bryan fired two shots. Unbelieving, we froze, and all at once a blackness burst through the branches. . . . I turned and let off two shots from the hip and then felt an explosion from behind. Another buffalo, wounded and down on its front knees, was circling with its hind legs before collapsing in a heap. Bryan lay between us a few feet away in the dirt, dazed. I hadn't seen him because he was run over by the first black, wounded

Rhino capture with Ken Randall
in Darajani, Hunting Block 29,
adjoining Tsavo East.
The captured rhinos were moved
into overcrowded Tsavo.

form. As he rolled over, yet another buffalo appeared, a cow with her head down, and he got off a perfect heart shot as she turned."

Man versus nature. It was a theme that would become Beard's primary focus. He wrote at the time: "In the fight of men and domestic animals against nature and her complex balances there is no compromise. In areas where there is a winner, the winner is absolute. In an environment ruled by nature's balances, man cannot play around without expecting unsavory repercussions. For instance, on the Fletcher estate not far from Colvile's, a successful anti-vermin fence had so protected the reproduction of Thomson's gazelles that seven thousand of them had to be shot. And when they built up again in a year or two, someone had to buy another seven thousand rounds of ammunition."

· · · · · · · · · · ·

In December 1961 Beard helped organize an ambitious foot safari into the NFD. He was to be accompanied by his friend from the States, Bill Du Pont, with whom he hoped to recreate the kind of walking safari the early hunters like Bror Blixen and Finch Hatton had taken many times. The two also hoped to set an example for highly selective shooting safaris in years to come, taking neither the side of tearful preservationists nor that of privileged sportsmen.

Beard and Du Pont arranged to meet up with eighty-four-year-old Philip Percival, then perhaps Kenya's most respected white hunter and one-time guide to Teddy Roosevelt. Percival spent five days with the safari, imparting his thoughts on Kenya's future to the young Americans. "You just can't interrupt a whole system of life and expect things to work out naturally," he told them. He gave Beard copies of a 1915 Roosevelt speech on conservation, which made it clear that populations expand and land does not: "When birds and mammals are left alone to reproduce at will within preserves—it will ultimately be necessary to cull them. The foolish sentimentalists who do not understand this are the really efficient foes of wildlife and of sensible movements for its preservation." These were mottoes Beard would carry with him for life.

This safari lasted several months, including Christmas spent on top of the Nguruman Escarpment. The hunters slept in the rain without benefit of tents and withstood hordes of mosquitos. Once, having run out of food, they lived on a porcupine until Du Pont, their best marksman, brought down a near-world-record Grant's gazelle. They baited leopards and lions with ostrich legs, and, accompanied by camels, hiked as far as twenty miles a day in search of elephants and rhinos. "Something new and strange was happening to us each day," Beard wrote of that time.

These travels exposed Beard to the harsh reality that he was seeing the last of such days in Kenya. Ranches were growing, populations were spreading, and hunting was soon to be outlawed. He was caught up in the romance of the professional hunter's life, a life in which survival of the fittest was more important than social security or union membership, but he was realistic about the future. He felt fortunate to have glimpsed the old Africa Karen Blixen wrote about—"the Africa at once hard and green, bloody and beautiful, eternal and ever new." Yet it was an image whose purity he knew could never be fully recaptured.

"The old spirit [of Africa] is hard to rouse," Beard wrote at the time, "and my occasional photographic successes are deceptive; they failed to show the airplane flying overhead or the fencing 100 yards behind the dead buffalo or the wounded lion. . . . In Nairobi the second-generation settlers, the saddest stratum of any immigrant group, live in the gap between white standards and a black world, maligning the coming life in Africa that *Uhuru* (Independence) will bring to them, and extolling the European pioneer world which only a few of them have really known. They appear curiously inert, their conversation a compound of distaste and regret and synthetic nostalgia. What their fathers fought and sweated for 50 years ago will soon be lost. The echoes in the glasses grow louder and the sense of futility becomes ominous."

. . . .

Beard's early experiences prompted him to look for a piece of Kenya to call home. When he first saw the land that was to become Hog Ranch it was accessible by a single grass track tramped down by the property's neighbor, American ambassador William Atwood. Beard had to stand atop his Land Rover to see the Ngong Hills outlined against the indigo African sky, but that was all he needed.

Giraffe, warthogs, dik-dik, bushbuck, waterbucks, leopards, guinea fowls, tree squirrels, mongoose, and a hundred varieties of exotic birds shared the lush bush on the strip of land, which sat on a ridge overlooking the Mbgathi Forest and the Masai Plains, facing west toward the Ngong Hills. At the turn of the century it had been the site of the last great battles between the Kikuyu and the Masai; in fact, a Masai *laibon* (holy man) is buried on the property in a stone grave next to an age-old cattle path.

Beard and his Nairobi lawyers lobbied for and received a presidential exemption for the purchase, because the land, considered agricultural, was too big a piece to be sold to a foreigner without one. Their argument was that Hog Ranch would become the headquarters for writers, filmmakers, and artists coming to Kenya to work on projects promoting the country's importance to the outside world. Beard envisioned a kind of Kenyan Yaddo—an artist's colony set on the outskirts of Nairobi. The property was

52

Bryan Coleman,
professional hunter,
doing control work on
the Lariak Estate,
with gun carriers,
1960

purchased for $20,000 from Mervyn Cowie, the founder and first director of Kenya's national parks. The money came from Beard's bank account and the pay he had earned for wrangling wild animals for a Coca Cola promotional film, directed by Nicolas Roeg, for an aborted product called Simba Cola.

After clearing a view of the Ngong Hills, Beard put up a string of safari tents along the ridge. He now had the perfect place from which to watch what he likes to call "the greatest show on earth."

· · · · · · · · · · ·

At first Beard hunted for pleasure, for sport. Then, in the mid-sixties, he hooked up with several of the numerous scientific outfits studying wildlife in Africa and from them learned the work of a slaughtering hunter, shooting hundreds of crocodiles, hippos, and elephants. The purpose of such hunting was to gather enough scientific evidence, after dissection, to better understand the animals' mating, reproductive, digestive, and aging processes. Game was plentiful; cropping made sense and was usually paid for by governments anxious to learn how to better manage the wildlife they hoped could one day pay for itself. Carrying his camera with him everywhere, Beard documented cullings of hippopotamus and elephant populations in Uganda, Tanzania, and the Congo—populations suffering from overgrazing and overcrowding. It was fascinating if occasionally dangerous work, and it introduced him to a wealth of wildlife professionals.

Organized in 1946, Kenya's national parks were run by a small, army-trained band of wildlife adventurers. Beard befriended them all—Mervyn Cowie, David Sheldrick, Peter Jenkins, Bill Woodley, and Ian Parker. He purchased property from Cowie; walked every step of the Aberdares with Woodley; lived for months with Sheldrick and his wife, Daphne; and attended drunken bashes with Jenkins, Parker, and the others after long days and weeks in the bush. They welcomed Beard for his outsider's humor, bush sense, and photographic achievements. Bill Woodley is both Beard's mentor and longest friend in Kenya; he remembers his young protégé in near-mythic terms: "Peter could run faster, walk further, shoot straighter than anybody. If hunting had lasted, he'd have been a great hunter. But he loved the bush . . . with or without a gun."

But Beard's fascination with big game went beyond that of the average hunter. One day in Uganda he was working with a pair of scientist/hunters, Ian Parker and Lionel Hartley, who were tracking and shooting elephants under the employ of the Nuffield Unit of Tropical Ecology. Late in the afternoon, armed with rifle and camera, Beard found himself on the opposite side of a hill from the others. As he listened to Parker and Hartley shooting, an angry bull came charging over the hill, directly at him. He stood his ground, for while the elephant appeared intent on skewering him, Beard curiously welcomed the experience. Meanwhile Parker and Hartley had come to the top of the hill, but were a hundred yards away. They both knew that a shot to scare or wound the big animal would be extremely difficult, yet Hartley shot once anyway. Miraculously, he dropped the angry elephant and it skidded to a halt, dead, ten feet from Beard. Beard's response was irritation rather than thankfulness, apparently unshaken by the charge but infuriated by the shooting. "I wasn't ready to run yet," he explained to Hartley, "it wasn't time." While the photographer admitted it may have been as close as he ever came to death in the bush, it was also perhaps his most exhilarating moment. Today his pair of hunting friends still shake their heads in amazement over his attitude and confidence.

Perhaps Beard's most thrilling months were spent in the company of a grizzled, eccentric rhino trapper named Ken Randall, a South African whom Beard still calls "the craziest man I ever met." "Traveling with Ken," he says, "was a gift to me and my camera."

Randall made a living on government contracts, catching rhinos in the hunting blocks and releasing the adults in Tsavo National Park. Beard remembers those chases—bouncing around on the running board of a Ford Bedford through the baobab and commiphera forests at forty miles an hour while attempting to lasso two-ton beasts—as "my first and best job in Kenya."

The rhinos—black and five feet tall at the shoulder—were difficult to spot from the ground in the dense scrubland. That meant that running into game was often sheer luck. Randall refused the assistance of airplanes, so ropers and spotters balanced precariously on the roof of the lead truck, which was followed by an ambush vehicle carrying a crew of ropers,

54

Ken Randall in
Darajani,
1964

Capture truck
and crew,
Hunting Block 29,
1964

diggers, pullers, and general helpers. Day after day the crew bumped along from dawn to dusk. When the chase commenced, the chief priority of the spotters was watching for burnt-out baobab stumps—vast black pits sometimes twenty feet across—into which the entire catching truck could disappear. Uncaring and slightly mad, the begoggled Randall would floor it over blind gullies, termite hills, boulders, rocks, acacia stumps, and thirty-foot trees. The windows of the truck had long ago been broken out; its cab was filled with tree branches, dirt, and leaves.

Once captured, the rhinos were trucked eighty miles into Tsavo, where they were disinfected, dewormed, deticked, and kept in log pens made from great tree trunks dug deep into the ground and wired together with sturdy cross beams. (On more than one occasion Beard paid natives out of his own pocket to construct the pens.) At first, each beast would hurl itself against its commiphera prison, shaking the pen and frightening the captors. The irony was that once released into their new home, nothing stopped the rhinos from running right back to their old stomping grounds in the hunting block. "This was conservation at its crazy best," Beard writes in *Zara's Tales*.

When not chasing rhinos Beard worked with Glen Cottar, who was building an out-of-the-way, fly-in safari camp on the nearby Athi River. A third-generation Kenyan by way of Texas, Cottar was a friend of Beard's from Nairobi; his intent was to sell "foot safaris for the more adventurous tourist," and he had been granted a special permit to take tours into the northern reaches of Tsavo. At eighty-three-hundred square miles, Tsavo was Kenya's biggest park, bursting with wildlife. Beard set up quarters at the end of the camp's runway and spent months building natural-looking rock blinds at water holes along the Tiva River to serve as overnight fly-camps—safe places to hide and observe lions and elephants. In his spare time he photographed game of all kinds. It was here that he was introduced to an ingenious local hunter named Galo-Galo Guyo, who would become his bush companion for the next twenty years.

The unlikely pair—the handsome patrician and the daring native hunter—spent six months camped along the Tiva, a dry sand river that snakes across the northern area of Tsavo. The most prominent of many elephant highways in the park crossed the Tiva at Kathamula. This was Galo-Galo's favorite stamping grounds.

Born near Voi in a small community of Waliangulus—infamous elephant trackers first discovered by Philip Percival, Bror Blixen, and Denys Finch Hatton—Galo-Galo was a traditional hunter. The skills he and his tribesmen possessed had only recently attracted attention because of the expanding safari business and the necessity of tracking big ivory. He was

Ken Randall
and Beard at
Darajani,
1968

Top
. . . . . .
Record
rhinoceros horn,
circa 47 inches,
Aberdares,
1964

Middle
. . . . . .
Rhino
on the run,
Serengeti,
1964

Right
. . . . . .
Capture truck
and crew, Hunting
Block 29, (adjoining
Tsavo East),
1964

also one of the first trackers employed during the Mau Mau emergency to investigate rebel murder scenes.

Beard learned much from his friend, who knew the intricacies of living in the bush: Galo-Galo could start a fire without matches in a minute and knew every plant and variety of wood. Once in the desert of the NFD, on one of many endless thirsty walks after elephant, the pair ran out of water. They were forced to dig a riverbed hole so deep that when water did gently fill in the bottom there was no way of getting at it; the sand caved in whenever they tried to reach down. Galo-Galo retrieved long sticks from the bush and after rubbing thcm in the palm of his hand was able to pull off the thin bark in the form of straws. These he joined together with a gummy sap until one straw about four feet long could be lowered into the water.

"Watching him was my education in the bush," Beard writes of his bushmate. "Whatever the hardship, he adapted quietly. On safari there was no better companion. He lived and survived with the game, kept the balance, did his honorable best. His was an authentic life of risks gladly taken with so few wants, intellectual in ways that are both practical and artistic. Most important of all, it was a life in balance with nature in which men do not become a plague on their environment."

When the pair camped on the Tiva, they spent day and night driving up and down the dry riverbed in Beard's Land Rover, photographing and exploring. They wandered across all of Tsavo North, from Daka Dema to Ndiandaza, and along the Athi-Tiva to Ithumba and the hunting block beyond. It was a special time for Beard, one that still stands out as the best of his life, if occasionally one of the most frightening.

One night Beard and Galo-Galo were joined by a rare visitor, a Kenya-born anthropologist named Robert Soper. They had spent the day digging an elephant skull out of the Tiva sand and had also discovered some ancient ochre cave drawings on the eastern face of the Yatta Plateau. Relaxing with Soper after a fulfilling day, they decided to celebrate at their sandy riverside camp with Beard's favorite bush treats—Ritz crackers, bread-and-butter pickles, Hellmann's mayonnaise, and a huge bottle of sake.

57

Charging lion in Loliondo, Tanganyika, 1963

Great Rift Valley
in the
Aberdares,
1967

58

The elusive
bongo,
Aberdares,
1968

Soper was glad to have stumbled upon the pair. He was low on food and had been reading early accounts of the man-eating lions that called this area home and that had once harassed the railroad builders as they crossed the desolate frontier at the turn of the century. The three men sat around the fire, the wind blowing, flames roaring. After, in his words, "ample drinking," Beard received a call from nature and walked thirty feet from the fireside into the pitch-dark night. As he "settled some dust" a blurred form came at him in slow motion; it was a charging lion, "like a weirdly silent bullet train erupting out of a high-speed wind tunnel." Beard stood paralyzed before yelling so loud that Soper, still warming his feet by the fireside, peed his pants. "My stomach went through the back of my neck and into my brain in an instant," says Beard, "creating a mental nightmare of speed and terror, one of those ultimate reminders of human puniness and frailty." Galo-Galo was instantly at his side, yelling and waving. Inexplicably the lion jammed on its brakes, reversed gears, and disappeared back into the bush.

. . . .

After combing Tsavo, Beard and Galo-Galo moved to the Aberdares, the premier park in the Highlands overseen by Beard's close friend Bill Woodley. Woodley allowed Beard to build a small cedar-log house in the middle of the Aberdares rain forest. The photographer's intent was to spend months roaming the park, taking pictures of its animals and teaching Woodley's rangers how to do the same. Then as now, Beard's infectious energy and charisma won him entrée to places granted few others.

As a personal goal, Beard set out to get a daylight picture of the ultra-elusive bongo, a seven-hundred-pound, dark-reddish, striped relative of the bushbuck and eland. It had not been done before and would not be simple; an assistant warden had recently left the park after twelve years and had never even seen one.

Beard's hut—built downhill, its parts numbered and then taken apart and carried six miles up into the Ruhuti River Valley—was constructed by Peter Wanjohe, who later built similar structures at Hog Ranch. It was positioned next to a small waterfall and stocked with camp beds, sleeping bags, weeks of food, Leicas and tri-x, and diary supplies (glue, scissors, magazines and newspapers, India ink, and pens). The hut had just one door and one window overlooking a natural salt lick. It was, Beard writes, "a Garden of Eden jungle paradise."

Joined by Galo-Galo, and at times several former Mau Mau generals and park rangers, Beard spent parts of six years exploring the Aberdares. Each day there produced something worth photographing: grunting forest hogs, long-haired silver-coated lions, midnight-black leopards, spotted serval cats, colobus-monkey–eating eagles, man-hunting elephants, exotic secretary birds, poisonous snakes . . . but no bongo.

Despite the missing bongo, the days hardly lacked for adventure. Once a wounded leopard fell out of a towering tree ten feet from the photographing Beard. It hit the ground hard, bounced, looked him in the eye, and exploded off into the forest, apparently unfazed by the eighty-foot drop. Beard photographed the biggest cape buffaloes of his career just one mile from his hut and found a near-world-record rhino on the moorlands at nine thousand feet. Accompanied by Galo-Galo and Mbuno, he climbed to the highest altitude of the Aberdares and found himself backed into corners by elephants, buffaloes, and rhinoceroses.

Also during these months he encouraged some of the growing network of fashion models he knew from around the world to join him in the bush, where he photographed them against a wilderness backdrop. In fashion circles those pictures, published in *Vogue, Harper's Bazaar,* and elsewhere, became his calling card. And on several occasions Beard captured parts of bongos on film—legs, sides, rear ends. He even managed to sneak in among large herds but still captured only bits and pieces. Finally, with Galo-Galo's help and a four-hundred-millimeter Leica lens, he squeezed off five or six shots of a giant bongo standing in the bush fifteen feet away.

"It was the most intense, most pregnant moment of all my wildlife crawlings and stalkings," he writes of that day. "After thousands of miles of hills and valleys and stinging nettles, all for this single vision, the wildest sight on earth, finally, a male bongo in the wild. Over the years no one has even noticed this picture. No one knows what it is. No one could ever guess the months and years of trouble that lay behind it."

The only flaw in Beard's Aberdares adventures was that they had to end. Returning to Nairobi was always a letdown. Once a quaint pioneer town, it had become like everywhere else: big, busy, and touristy, full of people. "Escape," says Beard, "was essential."

. . . .

The most tangible result of all these early adventures was *The End of the Game.* Initially Beard had envisioned it as a book of photographs detailing the fading Kenya he had seen, but when published it included considerable text—the fresh, stirring, if occasionally naive, insights of a young man caught up in the excitement of the time and his first extended stay in a great and mysterious land. He had met many of Kenya's most grizzled and respected characters, and in a sense, due to his quick intimacy with them, their loss became his loss, too. The book was more a lament for the good old days than it was a document of human mismanagement or the disastrous future waiting in the wings.

The End of the Game included a brief history of Karen Blixen's Africa and firsthand accounts of Beard's own travels. Begun in 1955, it was completed in 1963 (Beard put the finishing touches on it during a stint as an actor, in a film called *Hallelujah the Hills* shot in South Londonderry, Vermont). It was a blend of all things Beard admired: quotes from *Out of Africa,* the history of Blixen and Finch Hatton and other leading explorers, his first photographs of animals in the wild, and illustrations, drawings, and marginalia by himself and others. It was designed with a friend and proofread by his Yale classmate Bart Giamatti. Viking accepted it, paying the first-time author an advance of $750.

When the book came out in the States it received high acclaim, most notably in a pair of *New York Times* reviews. J. Anthony Lukas called it a "handsome and eloquent book . . . lamenting the passing of the old Africa," and Eliot Fremont-Smith said it was "a magnificent, haunting volume . . . a memory of the past, a record of the present, and an image of the future." At twenty-five, Beard's wunderkind reputation was official.

Elephants
in the Aberdares
Moorlands,
1968

Not surprisingly the book's publication was met with mixed feelings in Kenya, particularly by the professional hunters. In 1963 Tony Archer and John Sutton came to Beard at the New Stanley Hotel with a rehearsed speech. Their message was "How dare you write this book that says hunting is over. You're not a hunter, you're a neophyte. What do you know about our business?" Beard found himself ostracized by some hunters, essentially for telling truths about Kenya's future that most were not yet ready to see in print. Beard felt his reporting was justified; he had spent time with and interviewed enough experienced hands to stand by his occasionally dire predictions. He certainly did not wither under criticism.

There were glimpses, too, of Beard's future when *The End of the Game* was published. When asked by Viking for comment on the book, Joy Adamson, of *Born Free* fame, responded in a note: "Peter Hill Beard's book is an interesting study of the transition of East Africa from the early pioneering days to Independence and how this effects the wildlife of these countries. I congratulate the author on his research . . . I wonder though why he chose the double-meaning and rather misleading title *The End of the Game* instead of using the quotation mentioned in the last paragraph of his book, 'Always Something New and Hopeful.'" This was not the last time Beard's pessimism would be questioned.

Perhaps the most prescient assessment was proffered by John James Ellis Palmer, Beard's dean at Yale. After the book's publication he told the 1961 graduate, "I've been thinking about this book of yours and I think you could do the 'end of the game' for the rest of your life."

FIVE

Beneath the plane, the elephant mass moved like gray lava, leaving behind a
ruined bog of mud and twisted trees. An elephant can eat as much as 600 pounds of
grass and browse each day, and it is a destructive feeder, breaking down many trees and
shrubs along the way. Some parks can absorb this damage, but one sees quickly how
an elephant invasion might affect more vulnerable areas. Ordinarily the elephant herds
are scattered and nomadic, but pressure from settlements, game control, and poachers
sometimes confines huge herds to restricted habitats which they may destroy.
The elephant problem—where and when and how to manage them—is a great
controversy in East Africa, and its solution must affect the balance of
animals and man throughout the continent. . . .

— PETER MATHIESSEN, *The Tree Where Man Was Born*

Tsavo I: The Beginning of the End

Beard's relationship with Tsavo, Kenya's biggest park, goes back to the
early 1960s, but it was cinched when he met the park's longtime warden,
David Sheldrick. They'd first met in 1962 at Tsavo, but it was a 1963 run-
in, in a hospital room in Nairobi, that made them friends.

Glen Cottar had been run over by a buffalo and badly gored. Sheldrick
and Beard turned up to visit their mutual friend. The warden challenged
the young photographer shortly after they said hello: "I understand you're
spending all your time up in the green Aberdares. What's the matter, can't
take the hot, dusty climes? Why don't you come and work at Tsavo?"
Properly challenged and considering it an invitation, Beard decided to take
him up on the offer. Within weeks he had moved into the warden's house
at Voi, where Sheldrick lived with his wife, Daphne (who until the late
1950s had been Bill Woodley's first wife).

Today the park is laden with memories for Beard. In fact, many of his
views on Kenya, wildlife, and overpopulation were formed here by the still
argued, so-called Tsavo controversy—one of the longest-running conser-
vation/ecology debates in the world. Beard was privy to the controversy's
beginning, middle, and end. He knew, worked with, and lived with all of
its players. The controversy shaped his understanding of man's relationship
with nature, taught him firsthand about the importance of population
dynamics, and provided the subject matter for his most powerful photographs. His role, though primarily as observer, also cemented his later
reputation in Kenya as documentarian as well as protagonist.

Elephants
along the Tiva River,
Tsavo North,
1965

On a crisp sunny day we head for Tsavo in a rented *kombi* (van) along the road that runs to Mombasa. Our plan is to spend a couple of weeks roaming the areas of Tsavo not open to the public. When Beard first traveled this road in the early 1960s it was a muddy path, albeit one with a rich history. Safaris going back to Teddy Roosevelt's time had set out over these same plains. Soon after leaving Nairobi we pass Wami Hill, where Roosevelt had shot his first lions in 1909 and where Philip Percival had his home. Twenty-five years ago this vista afforded a horizon broken only by acacia trees, foothills, and grassland; today the roadside is spotted with signs of "progress": farms, petrol stations, billboards, warehouses, and the dung-and-stick homes of the Africans whose population is spreading rapidly beyond the limits of the cities.

Our destination on the first day is Mtito Andei (Place of Vultures), home to the warden of Tsavo West, Bill Woodley. This is Woodley's last week with the park system after forty-three years, so we know in advance that our visit will be filled with reminiscences and sadness. Woodley is one of Kenya's best-known bushmen and Beard's oldest friend in Kenya. He is being forced out of the only job he knows, and his future is uncertain. Though born in Kenya, he carries a British passport. In the continuing Africanization of Kenya's democracy, he is being replaced by a native. There is no pension waiting, no retirement fund. Saving money for retirement was never a priority for the sixty-five-year-old, who went to work in the national parks the day they were formed in 1946.

Woodley greets us at the door dressed in faded pressed greens. He has just flown in from blood-testing a rhino in the middle of the park, and the cool, spacious two-story brick house is filled with young park rangers. Ruth, his wife of thirty years, sits in a chair looking out toward Mount Kilimanjaro, which rises just over the horizon in Tanzania. From her chair, beyond the double glass doors that lead to the cement veranda, zebras, buffaloes, impala, warthogs, and even an occasional elephant can be observed as they drink from watering holes Beard and Galo-Galo Guyo dug in 1978. The view from the second-story sleeping porch is of one of Africa's greatest landscapes. In sight fifty miles away are the great volcanic ridges of Kichwa Tembo, Kibo, the main peak of Kilimanjaro, and the Chyulu Hills.

The Woodleys' home is a monument to a life spent in the bush: trophies, plaques, and photographs of elephants, buffaloes, and family. Books and whiskey are neatly arranged on the bar, and the BBC is tuned in day-long. A telegram to Bill from Prince Charles is proudly displayed. Glass-topped coffee tables bear early Beard photos from the Aberdares. An autographed photo of Mick Jagger signed "To Ruth, Love Mick" (a memento arranged by Beard) hangs next to a picture of her wallowing with elephants in the mudhole out front.

"You know, I introduced Peter to Kenya," says Ruth as she and Beard embrace. She had come to Kenya in the mid-1950s—like most, enchanted by the wildlife she'd heard so much about back home in London. She met Beard in 1960 when he approached the Ker & Downey kiosk where she worked. He wanted a safari, and she drove him straight to the Aberdares, where her boyfriend, Bill Woodley, was then warden. The trio have been fast friends ever since, and you learn most about Beard when he is in their company. His seniors by ten years, for nearly thirty years they have been his family, in a sense his surrogate parents.

Eland and elephants on the Tiva River, 1965

Bill Woodley is cut from classic colonial cloth. From the time he was a child, shooting gazelles for dinner near his mother's home on the Athi Plain, he was enthralled by Africa and the bush. His father died when he was nine, and the men young Bill chose to replace him were among the best white hunters of the day. Woodley learned from them and eventually shot for ivory and for money. He even shot men.

Hunting men was an experience he gained during his several years fighting the Mau Mau in the Aberdares with the Kenya Regulars. In 1952 Kenya's colonial leaders declared a state of emergency in response to the Mau Mau uprising. Woodley moved from Tsavo, where he had been assistant warden, back to the Aberdares. There he joined a military unit that used captured poachers first as trackers, then as accomplices, in the counterinsurgency known as "pseudoterrorism." In this practice a tracker led white officers to a group of Mau Mau hiding high in the hills. He initiated contact while the white officers, their faces painted black, hung back. At his signal the officers pulled guns from under their coats and opened fire on the rebels.

Bill Woodley was part of a small elite, kin by blood and marriage and vocation, that for twenty-five years dominated Kenya's national parks. At one time his jurisdiction was over one-third of the entire area of Kenya's park system.

Today half his stomach is gone to cancer and he's blind in one eye. When he and Ruth leave their park home, they'll move into a small house next to a gas station. Ruth is threatening to move back to England. Bill, who has never lived anywhere but in the bush, says he'll live in a cave rather than leave Kenya. Beard and many other old friends are trying to raise money to help them.

Beard's relationship with the Woodleys is unique. Late one night during our stay at Mtito Andei he kneels at the foot of their armchairs, working on his diary, reading to them from his favorite clippings. When Bill sneezes Beard runs for tissues. When Ruth needs a fresh drink, he fixes it. In their company it is as if he's come home again. He is humble, quiet, and mostly respectful in their presence, unlike his more typical boisterous around-the-campfire self.

The two men spend hours talking about their shared years in the bush, spent mostly roaming Tsavo and the Aberdares. They obviously miss the day-long hikes, the hunt, nights around the fire, the camaraderie. "Now I get up in the morning, and I don't know what to do," says Woodley. He is frustrated and depressed and worries that Kenya's future is as dire as his, predicting that droughts and the expanding human population will decimate the parks within the next generation. The sole bright side to his days is that two of his three sons are following in his footsteps. His eldest son, Bongo, is currently a warden in the Aberdares; his youngest son, Danny, is a warden at Tsavo East. (Benjamin, his middle son, serves in the British Army.)

Danny is at Mtito Andei when we arrive and will be our guide into the far northern reaches of the park his father helped to survey beginning in 1948. Dapper in a maroon beret and camouflage shirt and pants, with a Belgian automatic rifle slung over his shoulder, he has brought along a half dozen armed rangers to escort us. We will be traveling through areas littered with poachers, areas not open to tourists.

If the reminiscing is about the good old days—best guns, biggest elephants, legendary piss-ups, higher-ups who never knew enough to leave the politics in Nairobi—the aura in the warden's house is representative of the "new" Kenya. Danny and his rangers spend most of their days on anti-poaching patrol, a distinctly paramilitary operation. Where his father carried big, single-shot rifles, Danny carries a submachine gun. When Bill Woodley chased poachers from the air, it was with the stick of a single-engine plane wedged between his knees as he shot out the window. When Danny spots poachers, he calls in a British Bell Ranger helicopter mounted with the latest high-tech weaponry. The park they've each devoted themselves to protecting has changed, too. What was once a forest of low, spreading acacia is now mostly wasteland, just scrub and red soil stretching toward the horizon that ends at Kilimanjaro.

The elephant known as Ahmed-of-Marsabit. Photograph by Beard in company of Bill Woodley.

Early the next day we set out on a tour of the park. During an eight-hour round-trip drive we see numerous Promethean vistas but just a smattering of wildlife. Bill Woodley keeps track on the back of a used envelope: twenty-five lesser kudu, a handful of oryx, a single buffalo, ten elephants, a dozen giraffe. Thirty years ago, when Beard first visited Tsavo with his camera, the park teemed with game, especially elephants and

Najma Beard,
Bill Woodley,
Zara Beard,
and Elui on their
1991 visit to
Tsavo

rhinos. Woodley remembers when the park held more than sixty-five thousand elephants and eight thousand black rhinos. Today there are fewer than four thousand elephants, and just a dozen rhinos live behind an electric fence, guarded by men with machine guns. Drought, mismanagement, human population growth, and poaching have squeezed the animal population, and the march of the *watu* (the people) continues—Woodley estimates that more than thirty thousand cattle are already grazing on parkland in Tsavo East. It is predicted that within twenty years most of Tsavo's wilderness will be populated by man, with the wild game preserved under zoo-like conditions.

. . . .

The day after our tour of Tsavo, we head north, in a jeep and a van, on a bouncing, day-long drive into the far northwest corner of Tsavo East. Our crew comprises Bill and Danny Woodley; Beard, his wife, Najma, and his daughter, Zara; myself; a young photographer from New York; and four rangers. Camp is made along the Tiva River near Kathamula, where Beard and Galo-Galo had lived for months at a time during those years he considered the best of his life.

Though we've been in the bush just a few days, Beard is blackened from the sun, his uniform reduced to a pair of cut-off khakis and sandals. (His feet are permanently cracked, black, and calloused from years of wearing nothing but sandals whether in the bush or in New York City.) He has not been back to this bend in the river for twenty-five years. Now, accompanied by Zara, he is retracing his steps along the dry riverbed, which is covered by the night tracks of lions, elephants, and buffaloes. "This was the ultimate playpen," he pronounces exuberantly while scooping a pit in the sand for Zara to swim in. He tends to be more enthusiastic, less cynical, when in the bush, away from the headlines and temptations of the big city. "This was Elephant City. We hid along the shore and watched ellies by the hundreds, each and every night."

Elui,
near exposed
roots of an old tree
near the Tiva River,
1991

Later we go catfishing with Elui, a five-foot, hundred-pound hunter who has worked with Bill Woodley since 1948. Posed with a ten-foot-tall, world-record female ivory tusk, Elui graces the cover of the first edition of *The End of the Game.* With Bill set to retire, Elui has now started to work and travel with Danny. In the evening the light from a blazing campfire silhouettes the tall doum palms that line the river against the moonlit sky. Beard leans back on his elbows and calls this setting "el paradiso." He and Woodley swap "closest calls." Beard remembers hiking with Dougie Collins and getting ahead of him by several miles. "I stopped to wash in a clear mountain stream, and Dougie fired a shot hoping to get my attention. The damn .375 slug landed in the stream ten feet from where I was." His next closest call was while shooting zebras at Lariak, when a .375 accidentally whizzed by his ear. Danny tops that by recounting the zebra hunt on which he shot off the tip of his own thumb while riding and shooting from the back of a bouncing jeep. Bill claims he has never been shot, simply because he is "too thin."

When Beard moved to Tsavo in 1964, with park warden David Sheldrick's blessing and encouragement, he carried special permission granted him by the park trustees to photograph wildlife, on foot, for *Life* magazine. He was also to photograph fauna and flora for technical books conceived by Sheldrick and his wife. Soon after moving into the Sheldricks' home, Beard felt like part of the family, a member of the park system's royalty. He spent his days building blinds around the park for Sheldrick and photographing. He also wrote to ammunition companies in the States, inquiring at Sheldrick's behest if it was possible to put the immobilization drug M-99 in the heads of bullets. Sheldrick was planning for the inevitable culling operation he knew would be necessitated by the growing elephant population inside the park's boundaries.

From September 1965 to February 1966 the twenty-seven-year-old Beard crisscrossed Tsavo on foot accompanied by Galo-Galo. It is impossible to underestimate the impact this experience had on him. He was seeing places and wildlife few people, and certainly only a handful of white men, had ever seen. He and Galo-Galo followed herds of elephants for days, hiding in baobabs and bush and photographing them as no one had before. They spied on prides of lion and blended into packs of buffalo and wild dogs. The pictures that resulted from those months are some of the most intimate glimpses of Africa's wildlife ever recorded. Shuttling between the bush and the warden's home, Beard showed the results to the Sheldricks as the films were developed. They loved the energetic young American and his work, and encouraged him at every step. In early 1966, however, a fissure began to develop between photographer and warden.

70

Bill Woodley and Beard,
Tsavo,
1991

One early February morning a ranger patrol found Beard's empty Land Rover on the side of a single dirt track near Ithumba Hill. They radioed Sheldrick, who launched an air search for the photographer, assuming he was lost. When Beard and Galo-Galo innocently returned to the Land Rover around noon, Sheldrick was waiting for them. Angry, he demanded that Beard leave the park for good, maintaining that he had told him he could get out of his vehicle only as long as he stayed near it and that under no circumstance could he stay in the park overnight. Beard argued that he'd been walking the park for months and had written permission from the chairman of the board of trustees.

Though Beard appealed his ejection to national parks chief Perez Olinda, who had replaced Mervyn Cowie in 1966, his special privileges were withdrawn. "After Sheldrick's blowup, the trustees decided I could enter and use the park like every other tourist," he remembers today. "Big deal."

Beard's take on Sheldrick's reaction is complex yet simple. It was not unlike a falling-out between father and son. "He freaked out because I was getting too friendly with 'his' rangers," says Beard. "He was extremely territorial and ultimately didn't want anyone getting too close to 'his' park." Bill Woodley, who was Sheldrick's assistant at Tsavo for ten years, backs up Beard's remembrance of the clash, adding, "David had a strong ego. As long as I knew him, I don't think I ever understood him."

Beard's *Life* assignment was eventually completed in the Aberdares, with Woodley's assistance, and the results were published in a special double issue in 1968. However, his contentious relationship with Kenya's most powerful warden never healed. In later years they had several heated confrontations when Beard was visiting Glen Cottar's riverside camp on the Athi River, which sat just inside park boundaries. It became an intensely personal feud, with Sheldrick threatening prosecution if he ever found Beard in the park and Beard daring him to catch him.

If the clash was indicative of Beard's lifelong aversion to authority figures, it was also a clue to just how protective, how territorial Sheldrick was about the park he regarded as his. Ultimately Tsavo suffered irreparable damage due in part to the warden's zealous overprotection. Beard's most famous photographs documented the year-by-year die-offs in Kenya's largest park, die-offs many attribute to Sheldrick's strangling mismanagement.

Tsavo Park, divided into east and west sections by the Mombasa Railroad, was created in 1948 because the area—racked by hordes of tsetse flies and other pestilence and permanently semi-arid—was considered unfit for anything else. As one of the park's first wardens Sheldrick looked

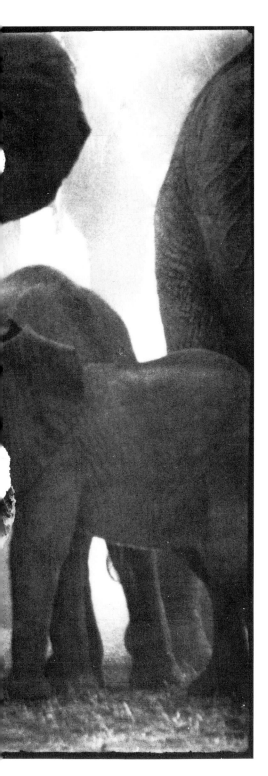

at its dry landscape, thickly vegetated by scrub and wild sisal, and knew that it could attract tourists only to see big game. He devoted years to building roads and culverts, providing year-round drinking water for visitors, and to conducting antipoaching campaigns against native hunters through a kind of antiguerrilla effort using Land Rovers, aircraft, and World War II repeating rifles.

To encourage the populations of wildlife, rivers were dammed and artesian wells dug. But this water worked too well, enriching the vegetation and leading to an over-abundance of thirsty elephants. By 1959 there were too many elephants for the food base—trees, plants, and grass—to sustain. Areas where the vegetation had once been so thick that elephants were visible only if they crossed a road began to resemble a lunar landscape. Too many elephants were threatening the woodland. Moreover, their old migratory routes had been cut off by a growing human population. It was felt by most, including Sheldrick, that a percentage of Tsavo's elephants would have to be eliminated, that is, culled, or cropped, in order to protect the population as a whole. Sheldrick therefore began to explore the specifics of the culling process.

One difficulty was figuring exactly how many elephants actually lived in the park and hence how many would have to be culled. In the early 1960s a British Army survey counted eighty-five hundred, which was about five thousand more than Sheldrick had guessed. As a result of that count, Sheldrick decided that five thousand elephants would have to be shot. Teams of skilled hunters would be sent into the bush to thin out the population. "At one point this was planned with rocket-bombs from the air, wasting ivory, skins and meat—a typical 'keep the books straight' British army response," writes Ian Parker in *Ivory Crisis,* his account of those years.

The decision to cull was what led Sheldrick to have Beard write American ammunition companies—particularly Du Pont—to see if tranquilizer could be drilled into the heads of bullets. "The tranquilizer bullets would be used to immobilize any wounded stragglers that escaped direct brainshots," says Beard.

In 1965 Kenya's National Parks director, Mervyn Cowie, refused to allow the culling, angering Sheldrick, who didn't like anyone telling him what to do in Tsavo and who feared that control of the park was slipping out of his hands. Seeking more opinions, Sheldrick, accompanied by Cowie's replacement, an African named Perez Olinda, traveled to Murchison Park in Uganda, where a successful, government-sponsored culling was ongoing.

The Ugandan government had contracted the well-respected Nuffield Unit of Tropical Ecology, based in London, to organize the culling at Murchison. In turn the unit had hired a Kenya-based, for-profit scientific team called Wildlife Services Ltd. to physically conduct the shooting. Wildlife Services was the brainchild of three close friends, experts in various realms of wildlife study: Ian Parker, Alistair Graham, and Alan Root (later joined by Tony Archer, Murray Watson, and Richard Bell). The company's philosophy was that zoological studies could be a successful, moneymaking business.

74

David Sheldrick (right) and Peter Jenkins

In its first years Wildlife Services took jobs ranging from collecting birds in the Western Indian Ocean for a museum to advising conservationists in Africa's westernmost country, Gambia. For a variety of clients they counted crocodiles, elephants, coots, hippos, crayfish, antelopes, rhinos, and ostriches, in Uganda, Kenya, Tanzania, Rwanda, Zambia, Malawi, and Botswana. They were hired to give advice on tourism; they drafted legislation; they made economic surveys; and they designed card index systems for faunal records. Their work extended into fisheries and even to advising filmmakers.

"But our name became most closely associated with 'cropping'—thus controversy," writes Parker in *Ivory Crisis.* "There is an ill-defined but widespread sentiment that to kill cannot be to conserve . . . a deep-rooted suspicion that anyone who embarks on commercial game-culling, cropping or killing may be a criminal and certainly not a conservationist. But animal management calls for the manipulation of populations."

Murchison Falls was perhaps Africa's best example of sound management by culling. The Uganda national park trustees had decided that the numbers of hippos and elephants in the national park should be limited; elephants had already reduced dense forest and a rich, mixed woodland to uniform coarse grassland. The Nuffield Unit sent Dr. Richard Laws, then regarded the world's premier large-mammal ecologist, to supervise the culling and carry out the scientific work. Wildlife Services was hired to kill four thousand hippos (out of an estimated fourteen thousand) and two thousand elephants (also out of an estimated fourteen thousand). For two years they shot hippos at night (selling the meat to Congolese butcher shops) and complete families of elephants by day, to the satisfaction of the Ugandan government.

The very same overcrowding affecting Murchison was simultaneously threatening the sanctity of Tsavo. Elephant populations were expanding, and as a result the woodlands were disappearing, replaced by grasslands that could not support the big animals. In the past elephants had been able to adapt to the diminishing browse by simply moving on to greener fields, thus allowing worn-out bushland to become revitalized. But this cycle of replenishment was no longer possible because of the farms and villages that now rimmed the park. The elephants had no place to go; if they ventured across the park's borders they were harassed, and even killed, by the expanding human population.

While Sheldrick and Olinda agreed that culling was the best thing for Tsavo, division among Kenya's park trustees made implementation of such a plan impossible. "For all the obviousness of what was happening, the authorities in Kenya seemed unable to decide on what action to take," remembers Beard. Eventually Sheldrick and Olinda decided to go ahead with a "test" culling. In 1966 they asked Dick Laws to come and work in the Kenya national parks as director of a Tsavo research unit, sponsored by a $350,000 grant from the Ford Foundation. His first request was that Wildlife Services be hired to take the sample of three hundred elephants, to be shot at Mkomazi in Tsavo East.

Beard was familiar with Wildlife Services; under its employ in the early sixties he had shot hippos, rhinos, elephants, and zebras in Uganda, Tanzania, and the Congo. The Wildlife Services team included some of the best and brightest wildlife scientists working in Africa in those days and, armed with camera or gun, Beard had proved himself a worthy bush companion. He had also assisted on the financial end, helping to convince big-monied Nairobi businessmen like Jack Block and Kenya's first vice president, Joseph Murumbi, to use their political and financial clout to nurture the young company.

As Beard remembers it, when Laws arrived at Tsavo he and Sheldrick became fast friends. Both were accomplished and at the top of their respective fields, and both were men of action. Sheldrick's ties with Tsavo, where he had labored for almost twenty years, were clear and deep. Laws arrived with an outstanding career in ecology behind him and justifiably considered himself competent to investigate the park's ecosystem.

Among Laws's first matters of business was to order a brand-new sample-counting by aircraft. This sampling, undertaken by biologist and elephant expert Murray Watson, provided the most accurate account to date and showed, much to Sheldrick's surprise, that there were actually more than forty thousand elephants using the park and surrounding area. Laws identified ten distinct populations of elephants and immediately suggested shooting three hundred out of each to help slow the booming and potentially destructive population growth. (Laws's three thousand was still two thousand fewer than Sheldrick initially had in mind.) Based on his studies at Murchison, Laws was convinced that if there were no culling, the elephants might soon destroy the food base in Tsavo. But he insisted that no culling take place until the Tsavo board of trustees approved a management goal and a long-range plan.

Soon the goodwill and respect shared by Sheldrick and Laws disappeared. They clashed on a number of issues, primarily Laws's conviction that the park had no long-range management policy. The truth was that any such plans were in Sheldrick's head, and he felt no need to write them down. Largely it was a clash between two strong egos, each intent on having his way. The relationship soured to an irretrievable level when Sheldrick suggested that Laws was encouraging cropping simply to steer business to Wildlife Service's Ian Parker and Tony Archer, who had pioneered such operations in Uganda and had an obvious monopoly.

The debate quickly deteriorated to name calling, pitting a pair of talented egotists against each other—the ex-military bush man versus the Cambridge-trained scientist. Sheldrick hated the fact that someone else had come into his park and was suddenly trying to tell him what to do to save it. He disagreed with and opposed Laws's "ten populations" theory and now argued against any further culling. (Wildlife Services had gone ahead with the shooting of the sample of three hundred elephants at Mkomazi.) In arguments he made to the national parks trustees, Sheldrick now claimed that rather than cull they should wait for a die-off that was destined to occur during the dry periods, which would bring the elephant population in line with the carrying capacity of the land. The weaker of the species would die, he contended, insuring that those that survived would be healthier. Ultimately the trustees sided with their veteran warden and his laissez-faire "nature can care for itself" approach. Laws and his team were asked to leave Kenya. ("Wildlife Butchers Forced to Leave" screamed the headlines of the local papers.) Irate over what he saw as Sheldrick's short-sightedness, Laws labeled the warden's claims that new grasslands would be able to carry current elephant populations as "fatuous nonsense."

Beard remembers the clash vividly. "While initially they were the best of friends, the struggle for authority killed their friendship. Two powerful men, each refusing to go along with the other, decided to stick by their guns for no other reason than to protect their egos."

Underlying the ego-filled clash were hints of future horrors to come. Laws predicted that thousands of elephants would die, but few listened to him. After leaving Tsavo and Kenya, with the elephant population still growing, he continued to repeat his charge that a policy of "heroic-romantic laissez-faire" as against long-term "scientific conservation" would lead to the disappearance or gross reduction of Tsavo's elephants. "The Tsavo elephant problem is a classical example of indecision, vacillation, and mismanagement," Laws wrote in 1969. "We can expect a series of dry years shortly, when the Tsavo problem will again assume manifest crisis proportions."

At the time Laws could not have predicted that, despite all of his scientific reasonings, the person who would finally focus world attention on the controversy in Tsavo would be neither a scientist nor a warden, but a photographer. Nor could Beard have predicted in 1966 that the Tsavo controversy—a classic case of man against nature and man against man—would be the seminal event of his photographic life.

78

Elephant before
Mt. Kilimanjaro,
1965

SIX

. . . .

*A violent gale blew unceasingly day and night . . . like an
avalanche . . . rushing into the deep basin of the lake sometimes
in terrific gusts. At times it was difficult even to stand, and
cooking and eating were conducted under disadvantages. Nothing
would stop on the table, the very tea was blown out of one's cup,
while the black sand and small stones got into the food and
filled one's bed at night.*

— ARTHUR NEUMANN

Harlem Comes to the Birthplace of Mankind

The day after we returned from our two weeks in Tsavo, Beard and I were at Nairobi's Wilson Airport rustling up a pilot, chartering a plane, and then flying off over the Great Rift Valley to Lake Rudolf, site of some of Beard's most wild and poignant adventures.

Our pilot and companion for the trek was a British novelist named Richard Cox. A former correspondent for the *Sunday Times* of London, he had been thrown out of Kenya in the late 1960s for landing his plane in a neighboring country without invitation. Out of diplomatic politeness, Kenya canceled his visa, and he went on to write speeches for the Aga Khan. When we met up with him he was researching his fifth novel, featuring a fictional Kenyan relief worker.

The bushy-browed Cox, with oh-so-rigid Britishness, was a potent contrast to Beard's devil-may-care approach to everything. He would spend hours each day making lists and—armed with protractor, calculator, and pencil—figuring and refiguring the minutes of flying time and fuel needs for the next day. He sweated madly in the pursuit of these details and chain-drank beer mixed with Sprite to stave off the desert heat.

With Beard as copilot, our days spent shadowing the border of Ethiopia and Kenya was an experience Cox will never forget. The photographer's childlike enthusiasm and curiosity can be infectious and charming. It can also be annoying, if occasionally maddening. Thankfully the two

Record keeping on Alia Bay.
One such crocodile photo was
included in Voyager II's
time capsule.

found some common ground, particularly since Cox had reported on Kenya during the early years of its major transformations. He maintained that the biggest mistake made by the framers of Kenyan independence was allowing elected officials to keep their hands in private business. The result has been massive, widespread corruption from the president down to policemen. Beard loves this kind of talk.

We were headed to one of the most isolated places on earth. Situated on the floor of the Great Rift Valley in northernmost Kenya, smack up against Ethiopia and the Omo River Delta, Lake Rudolf is a fearsome place of volcanic rock, smoking craters, windblown sand, and wild nomads. (In deference to history, the 155-mile-long lake will be referred to here as Lake Rudolf, as it was called when Beard lived on its shore. In the wholesale Kenyanization of the country in the early 1970s, the name was changed to Lake Turkana, a change he refuses to acknowledge. Still today various tribes know the lake by different names: The Samburu call it *Basso,* "the Big Water beyond Nyiru"; the Turkana know it as *Aman* and the northern tribes as *Gallop.)* Once connected to the Nile River, the lake is now cut off from virtually everything. Two degrees off the equator, it rarely receives any rain and year round its shores are haunted by hot dry winds that blow day and night and average temperatures of 120 degrees.

We flew over tin-roofed shacks and *shambas* (thatched huts) to reach the lake shores lined with flamingos and graceful, soaring white-winged ibises. Ashen-gray volcanoes anchor the south end of the lake; its lone three islands—North, South, and Central—stood out like fortresses. A miraculous if barren scene spread out a thousand feet below the shadow of our small plane. A gathering of thirty hippos (looking, as Cyril Connolly described, like "prosperous African churchmen, Harlem revivalists stepping into their limousines") barked along the shore. Camels and bone-thin cattle plodded in a separate, single file toward drinking water. Longboats were being poled back from a day's fishing. The only color other than shades of brown and blue was the red of the robes of the Turkana tribespeople, who from this altitude looked like drops of blood in the sand.

Hidden beneath the shimmering surface of the so-called Jade Sea swam two-hundred- to three-hundred-pound Nile perch and some of the biggest crocodiles on the planet. Above soared the most varied bird life in all of Africa. Beard turned and, gazing out the window, called Lake Rudolf "the most rapturous place on earth."

It *is* the biggest permanent desert lake in the world, with a shoreline longer than the whole of Kenya's 530-mile seacoast. Today, however, it is a mere sliver of its former expanse. Recent drought years and irrigation projects in southern Ethiopia have seen the inflow dry up, so that now the water level is at its lowest point in living (or passed-down) memory. Like a gigantic sump, with rivers flowing in but with no outlet, the lake sees a staggering three meters average depth of water evaporate from its surface each year, dropping it nearly a centimeter a day. As a result, it is alkaline. Less than ten thousand years ago, it was 150 meters deeper and spread south as far as Baringo; it once fed the headwaters of the Nile, which accounts for the presence still of its huge Nile perch. Not so long ago the lake was also home to between ten thousand and twenty thousand Nile crocodiles, which have been essentially wiped out by gill net fishing.

It is thought that *Homo sapiens* originated near Lake Rudolf. Skeletal fossils nearly three million years old—discovered by the wife-husband-son anthropologist team of Mary, Louis, and Richard Leakey—show that the evolution of man from his apelike ancestors probably took place along these rocky shores. Those bones have earned the lake its reputation as the birthplace (or cradle) of mankind.

The lake was first seen by white men on March 6, 1888. An ambitious Austrian count named Teleki von Szek came by foot safari across almost the whole of East Africa accompanied by three Swahilis, six guides, eight Somalis, fifteen *askari* (guards), over two hundred porters, and a faithful biographer, Lieutenant Ludwig von Hohnel. It was a hellish journey over steep precipices, insurmountable blackish-brown lava rock, and narrow valleys cluttered with stones, prehistoric debris, and deep loose sand. The sun caused a nearly intolerable glare, sand whipped in their faces, and the constant wind nearly blew the loads off the men's heads. The lake itself was an undrinkable brackish expanse rippling with whitecaps. Teleki named the lake for the neurotic crown prince of Austria, who later committed suicide after shooting his mistress in the head.

Since its "discovery," Lake Rudolf has been visited by only a few outsiders. Explorer Arthur Neumann reported that fierce gales threw him to the ground when he was there in the early 1900s. Sir Vivian Fuchs, who led an expedition to the lake in 1953, lost two of his companions when they tried to reach South Island in a collapsible boat and were never seen again, their craft most likely overturned by angry hippos. In the 1950s Robert Maytag, heir to the American washing machine fortune, organized an expedition to the lake; today his boat, specially designed and built in Canada, sits on the lake bottom. Recognizing the dangers the lake held, the natives of the region rarely ventured far from shore. When they did, it was aboard rafts made of two or three logs.

Beard and biologist-writer Alistair Graham visited the shores of Lake Rudolf many times during the mid-sixties, hunting, dissecting, and documenting the lives of crocodiles.

Near the tip of the western shore, we circled our small plane over the only lodge on this side of the lake, near the small village of Kalokol. We were trying to raise someone, anyone, since we would need a lift from the airstrip, which is a half hour away. Beard tried to convince Cox to set the single-engine Cessna down on the beach (as Alistair had done dozens of times), but Cox was far too cautious to respond to Beard's spontaneity. As a result we fried on the cement airstrip in 120-degree heat for two hours, waiting for the only vehicle in town to be alerted and retrieve us. After a longboat ride across the bay to the otherwise deserted Turkana Fishing Lodge—fifteen rustic cabanas set high on the beach—we drowned ourselves in cold beers and ate freshly smoked perch.

Sitting at the bar Beard recognized half the Turkana employed by the lodge. Some had worked as skinners during the crocodile hunts when they were just boys. Now, wearing polyester pants and smocks, they had steady employment at the lodge, which in the winter months caters to a crowd of mostly East Indians who come from Naivasha and Nairobi for desert holidays. As we talked, the one-eyed bartender, a Bic pen stuck through his short-cropped hair, eyed us suspiciously. They are still not used to light-skinned visitors here and are curious about why we've come.

The lodge, built over twenty years ago, stands on a spit of high beach that once overlooked Ferguson's Gulf, which is adjacent to the lake and linked to it by a short natural canal. A fortress-like wall rises in front of the lodge, intended to stave off rising tides. Today it sits forlorn, cracked and unnecessary—the lake doesn't come within four hundred feet of it.

Drought and diversion have reduced the four-mile-wide Ferguson's Gulf to a waterless sandbox, but interestingly, when Beard and Graham first visited here in 1963, an elderly Turkana chief had spun tales of a hundred years before when you could walk across it. At the time no one believed him, since the gulf appeared to be deep and permanent. Now it is obvious that his story was not myth but merely reporting on one of nature's cycles.

From the cement veranda we could see Turkana fishermen hauling in their nets, tall, elegant women wringing their wash in the shallows, and dozens of young children running up and down the beach. The moon was rising as the fishermen began to pole their rough-hewn boats to shore. The orange sun disappeared quickly, etching the surface of the flat black lake with streaks of gold. It was a scene that had been repeated day after day, uncorrupted for centuries.

. . . .

85

Boran woman,
1962

"It seemed to us that rather than abandon the world's last great crocodile population to the whim of man, to be exterminated in the name of inevitability, we might first inquire a little into their lives. Perhaps as a result of our work the existence of crocodiles, which has been a fact of nature for 170 million years, would take on a renewed significance." That was how, in 1965, Alistair Graham summarized his reasons for wanting to come to Lake Rudolf to study its crocodiles.

With his Wildlife Services partner Ian Parker, Graham had been hired by the Kenyan Government to study the Nile crocodile, a previously ignored creature. Their job was to assess the biological status of the lake's crocodile population in order to help the game department shape a policy toward an animal traditionally despised as a dangerous pest. Though the company had been contracted by the government, there was no money to pay for the survey. That meant Wildlife Services had to finance its study out of what it could get for the skins of the five hundred crocs to be killed for investigation. The shortage of funds sent Parker on to other projects, and Beard signed on as Graham's partner. "His devil-may-care manner was a tonic for the rest of us, though he clearly confirmed the Turkanas' suspicion that all white men were completely crazy," wrote Graham at the time.

The goal of the study was to find out as much as could be learned by observation and dissection, living tooth-by-armor-plate with the biggest crocodile population left on earth. "We knew nothing of crocodile population dynamics," wrote Graham, "their food and shelter requirements, the scale of births and deaths within a population, the factors influencing natality and mortality, the structure in terms of age and sex, and so on. Why, for instance, did three-quarters of Rudolf's crocs concentrate on the northeast shore?"

At the time, world demand for crocodile skins was increasing while the supply was dwindling. The Okavango swamps in Botswana had been cleaned out; the Uganda Game Department had virtually exterminated crocodiles in that country except for a population of about two thousand at Murchison Falls; and the last few Ethiopian rivers with good crocodile populations were being ruthlessly hunted. This increasing scarcity meant an ever-rising value on Nile crocodile hides. Graham hoped that with the help of his observations, maybe Lake Rudolf's crocodiles could be intelligently exploited and skillfully managed rather than simply wiped out.

Graham, Beard, and half a dozen Turkana helpers set up camps on either side of the lake, at Ferguson's Gulf, Moite, and Alia Bay. At the time the region was menaced by *shifta*—roving outlaws hostile to Kenya and sympathetic to the neighboring Somali Republic. Because of the risk of banditry the scientific team kept as mobile as possible while on the east side, storing gear when not in use on the west side at Kalokol. This meant crossing the lake every month, for skins had to be turned into cash regularly in order to keep the study going. Continuity was essential, so for a solid twelve months in 1965–66 Beard and Graham rarely left the lake.

Beard's main assignment, other than photographing carcasses, was hunting day and night. His limitless energy and enthusiasm were indispensable to a sometimes flagging project; often he managed to turn mishaps into laughter.

Under Graham's tutelage, Beard's wildlife education grew. Dick Laws had introduced him to the realities of population dynamics; Alistair offered Beard graduate studies. ("A great deal of what masquerades as wildlife research is really self-indulgence on the part of donors and acceptors of 'grants' concerned, consciously or not, more with bolstering the myth of a pristine, totally unfathomable nature than with explaining its workings," wrote Graham.) Today, sitting on the cement veranda of the Turkana Lodge, Beard says that the lessons he learned in his years working on these shores can be reduced to one simple sentiment: "Crocodiles are a hundred and seventy million years old; man is two to three million years old. In that incredibly short time we have nearly destroyed or totally jeopardized the global habitat. We're a disease on earth, a virtual cancer on the once-healthy planet."

. . . .

During one of Lake Rudolf's inestimable sunsets Beard and I take a stroll through the Turkana village that sits in the sand near the fishing lodge, led by one of the skinners-cum-busboys. A crowd follows, mostly young boys, smooth-skinned and smelling of wood smoke, who introduce themselves by their Christian names—Michael, Jackson, Matthew, James—and compete to hold our hands. They ask for pens, sodas, T-shirts, and money to buy books. Trailing behind, carrying our shoes and the rocks, shells, and bones Beard invariably accumulates on any walk, they whistle and sing, happily oblivious to more civilized concerns. Many of the natives, dressed only in *kikois*, or loincloths, recognize Beard, though it has been more than twenty-five years since he introduced them to the camera. One boy, born long since Beard was last here, inexplicably calls him "The Holy Man." Beard blushes. We learn that one of the women we're seeking, a young girl named Akaeyee, whom Beard photographed in 1965, has died.

Beard points to where Bob McConnell's thatched hut once stood. At one time it was the only building for hundreds of miles. McConnell, an Englishman who had come in the early 1960s to fish and to educate the natives, spoke perfect Turkana. He discovered that the natives talked about only two things: food and sex. His most important job was teaching the

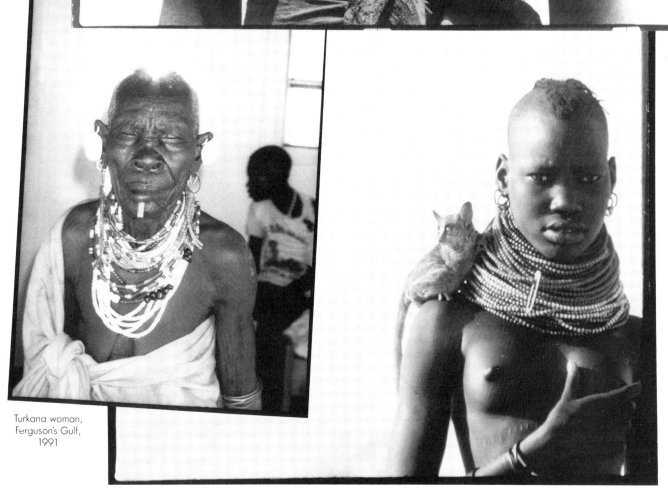

Turkana woman
with scars,
1967

Boiloin,
1965

Turkana woman,
Ferguson's Gulf,
1991

Turkana to fish. Before his arrival they had been malnourished and actually starving, scared of the murky, crocodile-infested waters, even though the lake held literally tons of food.

We are looking for a woman Beard remembers photographing when she was sixteen. Her name is Boiloin, and he has learned that she is now the mother of six. When we find her, in a dung-and-doum-palm hut, she covers her mouth with her hand out of surprise and her bare breast with her *kikoi* out of modern-day modesty. Her hair is cut to the scalp, a thick pile of necklaces wrap around her elongated neck, and one-inch ceremonial scars cover her shoulders and stomach. She is barefoot, her toenails all but rotted away. She is probably forty. She introduces us to her children, including a son named Peter (Beard quickly blames that on missionaries, not himself). The setting sun glows warmly as he talks quietly with the gathering crowd in Swahili. This is where his true self shines. These people revere him and treat him like a long-lost friend.

The village has changed considerably since the days Beard lived nearby. There are four churches and three schools now. Kalokol has a post office and a row of mud-walled shops, a kind of African strip mall. When Beard first visited here the people wore little or no clothing. Now missionaries have spread the word that nudity equals savagery, and as a result young and old are dressed in polyester pants and T-shirts, most ripped nearly to shreds. By appearance, these people would easily fit in East Los Angeles or the Bronx. It is another of the old places Beard remembers fondly and is sickened by today. He blames missionaries and aid workers. "First we screwed them with medicines and bribes; now they're screwing themselves. Why didn't we just leave well enough alone? Why did we have to missionize and compromise them, turn them into beggars? They were just fine until we barged in."

. . . .

Horrendous conditions nearly made the Graham/Beard crocodile study impossible. The lake is deceptively treacherous; its winds average twenty to thirty miles per hour and whip up on a whim to fifty or sixty. "It's just like an ocean," says Beard. "We often saw crocs being tossed about in ten-foot waves." On the first day of what was to be more than a year on the lake, their boat sank. During the course of their study its replacement, Alistair's nineteen-foot converted lifeboat known as "The Curse," was swamped four times, and eventually it sank, too.

For shelter Beard and Graham designed blow-through canvas sheeting rigged on steel frames; tents would have been too heavy, too wind-resistant, and unbearably hot inside. Because these open shelters offered the only shade, they served as dissection room/bedroom/storeroom. Sand was in everything, and flies were a major annoyance. By day the black volcanic

Alistair Graham
asleep in the
Alia Bay shelter

shore was furnace hot, the heat interrupted randomly by violent whirlwinds that tore through the camp like miniature tornadoes, scattering anything not weighted down with stones.

Their diet was mostly catfish, supplemented by Ritz crackers, Hellmann's mayonnaise, bread-and-butter pickles, condensed milk, and a few treasured tins of grapefruit. Soup was concocted from grand-sounding packets like egg-drop, mushroom, and chicken noodle, but the vile alkaline water polluted everything. Black volcanic sand was in every mouthful of catfish, perch, turtle, and zebra. "The cook's forte consisted of dropping slabs of catfish, some fat, and plenty of sand into a pan and heating it for an indeterminate period," remembers Beard. "The result was then dumped,

wordlessly, before us. There was, to be sure, nothing to say." The natives existed primarily on crocodile meat. (Beard: "I have eaten nearly every kind of wild animal meat and found all of it good with the single exception of croc. It is an oily, pungent flavor however cooked, cut-up, or disguised.") Occasionally they were treated to Nile turtle or croc eggs.

Beard's and Graham's teeth turned brown from drinking the alkaline lake water, which Beard claimed tasted "like melted jellyfish." Hyenas and lions stole and ate several fresh croc carcasses even though they'd been anchored well offshore. Scorpions crawled into sandals, damp-skinned toads were found in every jar and metal box, and poisonous, night-traveling carpet vipers hung from tent frames. The investigators could not have picked a more difficult and dangerous location for a scientific survey.

· · · · · · · · · · ·

Our days at Rudolf are spent flying over and around the lake, up and down its coastline. We set the Cessna down at a number of desolate spots, including Alia Bay, where Graham and Beard had camped for many months. (Beard also spent months there in 1969 with his good friend Bill Holden and the film crew of *Journey to the Jade Sea.* He'd met Holden in Africa in 1960, when the actor was starring in *The Lion,* being filmed at the Mount Kenya Safari Club. Beard was hired as a technical adviser on *Jade Sea.* Each weekend the film crew would fly off to the coast to escape the lake's nightmare conditions, but Beard stayed behind, treating himself to day-long Stones and Dylan concerts, the parties lasting until he ran out of diesel fuel for the generator and the batteries for the cooler and the tape deck went dead.)

Beard and Graham's camp at Moite, despite its bleakness, gained a certain peacefulness from its sheltering mountain; there were even a few thorn trees and some stunted palms. By comparison Alia Bay was nothing but a windswept stretch of lava, with no vegetation or shelter of any sort. When we land there, the noise of the plane sends a herd of chocolate-colored topi scattering. A jeep from the recently constructed ranger station roars in our direction.

When we reach the shoreline, accompanied by a pair of KWS rangers, we find crocodile and zebra carcasses, recently devoured by lions. Just offshore a half dozen hippos belch and snort, looking like bulbous subma-rines. Pelicans and flamingos stroll along the beach. The fields of tall yellow grass hide small bands of Grevey's zebras, oryx, and Grant's gazelles. A solitary giraffe stands silhouetted against the horizon; an ostrich and a gerenuk watch us as we walk to the highest point overlooking the lake. Beard is mystified by the geographical changes since his last stay here. Shingle Island, a mile and a half offshore, where he had spent days and nights hunting crocodiles, has totally disappeared, but the grassy area where we stand had then been under water.

Paralleling the shoreline are a dozen ramshackle buildings, built of faded plank, cement block, and corrugated tin, and patched with mud and cow dung. The area has been made a national park since Beard was last here, and fourteen rangers and their families, goats, and chickens now call Alia Bay home. Their presence mars the once-pristine shoreline. One of the magical places in the world, home to a diverse abundance of wildlife and the very birthplace of mankind, has been destroyed by the slapdash construction of a row of offensive shacks. We ask the rangers why they are based here and they reply "to catch poachers"; in the next breath they admit they haven't seen one in months. We ask them to identify a crocodile vertebra and they hold it in their hands, studying it, and confess they don't know. One of them cannot identify an oryx standing a hundred feet away. "Another confirmation the world is crumbling, even in this most remote spot," groans Beard.

Alia Bay was where Beard and Graham engaged in some of their best hunting. Using .270 silver-tipped bullets, they learned much about crocodiles simply by pursuing them. Their goal was to shoot a minimum biometric sample of five hundred during their stay, or forty to fifty each month. At the time it was estimated that there were thirty thousand crocs in the lake, which gave them plenty to cull from.

It proved an arduous task. They needed a random sampling of ages and therefore shot any adult available. The bigger, older, and smarter, the better, but "monster pebbleworms"—as Beard and Graham referred to those over thirteen feet long—were rare. Most ranged from six to ten feet.

Hunting day and night was a necessity. "We had hoped to hunt from a boat, but the wind ruled that out," wrote Graham. "Then we found that because the lake was shallow a long way out, most of the crocs were out of range of a hunter walking along the water's edge. So we had to go in after them. Our technique was for one of us to walk in front with a torch, followed closely by a rifleman. Behind him came one of the men to tow our kills along. This was necessary because if we left them on shore they were quickly stolen by the lions or hyenas that followed us when we were hunting at night.

"The torch bearer would cast around for crocs, whose eyes shone red in torchlight. Finding a suitable one, we would try to approach without alarming the wary animal, which more often than not would silently submerge and disappear. Once down, a croc can last up to an hour without breathing. Although the light dazzled the crocs, many things worked against us to warn them of danger. It was essential to keep downwind, for their sense of smell is extremely good. Their hearing is keen, too, and this was our greatest problem, for the ground underfoot was seldom easy to traverse soundlessly. Mostly it was a vile ooze studded with sharp chunks of lava and rocks. Every now and then someone would plunge into a soft patch, for it was a constant struggle to keep upright. Many were the crocs lost at the last moment as somebody subsided noisily into the lake. Scattered about were hippo footprints, deep holes in which the lava chunks clutched at you like gin traps. A shoe torn off deep beneath the mud was almost impossible to retrieve without alarming a croc floating a few feet away."

Close calls were an almost daily occurrence. Graham shot one big croc, walked up to it, and was surprised when it began thrashing about, snapping its jaws viciously. Stumbling, he felt it whip around and its jaws close on his leg. He let out a muffled howl and managed to wrench his leg clear with no damage other than deep gashes. On another night he was bitten by a spitting cobra. Luckily it was only a scratch; he jumped aside at the last second and the fangs only grazed him, leaving two teeth marks about a centimeter apart as the sole evidence of the strike; small tracks of blood trickled from each tiny wound. Beard remembers the twenty-minute journey back to camp as chilly and uncertain. "We all expected him to keel over, dead," he says.

On yet another night a twelve-footer came like a torpedo from more than thirty yards offshore straight at the flashlight, which Beard was holding. Graham was so surprised that his two or three shots failed and then the gun jammed. "Scared stiff, I held the flashlight out to the side and ran around in tight circles," wrote Beard at the time, "waiting for a finishing shot. Alistair hurled his rifle to the ground, took out his trusty Colt .45 and at point-blank range, fired again and again. The scaly leviathan was on auto-pilot and it took several loads to weigh it down with lead." Another night one of their native hunters was grabbed from behind by a ten-foot croc on Central Island. He managed to get away after a grisly tug of war that sent him to the hospital in Nairobi with massive injuries.

Animals weren't the only beasts Beard and Graham had to watch out for. Merille, Rendile, and Boran tribesmen passed by their campsites many nights, looked them over, and kept walking. The researchers were lucky. In Loingalani, near the southern tip of the lake, Somali bandits with automatic weapons raided the lake's only fishing lodge. A Catholic priest was killed, the lodge's manager shot in the back of the head, and an Italian driver speared and skinned.

For an efficient kill, crocodiles had to be shot in a brain region about two inches square. Beard became expert at sneaking up on them to get his brainshot. During the day he would float within five feet of them, hidden

Beard
stalking crocodiles
in Alia Bay

behind a black inner tube and masked by a camouflage skin of fresh mud and pelican dung.

"It was an adaptation of the old croc hunter's trick of crawling towards a 'basking' croc, very slowly, concealed behind a bush which he pushes in front," wrote Graham. "In his variation, Peter swam towards sleeping crocs pushing an inflated inner tube along in front. The gun lay across the tube, wrapped in *kikois*. When in range he inched himself up onto a patch of beach and fired. The method was highly successful, with the crocs astonishingly unsuspecting. His greatest triumph came one afternoon when he actually nudged a 'watchstrap'—a smallish crocodile—out of the way with the rifle barrel to get a shot at a big one beyond. Another time he stopped a nine-footer through the open mouth of a smaller one next door." In spite of the excitement, it was cold and dangerous work. Many crocs, far from being afraid, were hostile and came for the hunter aggressively. Advancing crocs drove Beard ashore on several occasions.

"A bigger problem," says Beard, "is that when you're shooting a crocodile at close range you can't always tell if it's dead. If your shot is a little bit off, he just gets knocked out. Then you dive down, pick him up off the bottom, and by the time you get to the surface he comes alive. That happened to us several times, once after we already had the creature in the boat. If I'd shot him, it would've put a hole through the bottom of the boat. We made it to shore with everybody sort of hanging over the edge."

Today he claims he hunted crocs "for fun and for the joys of dissection," certainly not for profit. Indeed, while they reaped a few grade-A skins, most had major flaws. The best were sold directly to Paris. It was a break-even adventure at best, one that could never have been profitable since each crocodile they shot then required many hours of work, skinning, dissecting, and analyzing.

Beard insists that proximity to danger was not one of his motives, but friends then and now insist he thrived on it. One day at Loingalani, his friend Van Someron watched Beard swimming well offshore. A croc took chase and Someron shouted. Beard didn't hear him, and as he swam to shore, the croc followed. Someron rushed to his tent for a gun, but by the time he got back to shore, the croc was a few feet from the swimmer—too close to shoot. Safely ashore, Beard's reaction was annoyance that he'd been unaware of the danger.

Throughout their times together Alistair was constantly amazed by Beard. "When Peter sees a dangerous situation, he has to get involved. What he likes most about Africa is to do your own thing there, a way of life you create with no plan. To Peter, something is creative only if it happens by surprise. He can't—won't—accept the normal responsibilities of society."

. . . .

The crocodile survey ended in typically Beardian fashion, with the sinking of "The Curse" September 17, 1966. On that day, three crocs short of five hundred, Alistair dropped Beard and a knock-kneed skinner nicknamed the Wildman on Shingle Island. They were to spend one last cold, windblown night hidden in trenches scooped out of the sand, waiting to shoot anything that came ashore early the next morning.

When Alistair returned in "The Curse" the next morning to pick up the hunters and the last three crocs, the wind was blowing twenty to twenty-five miles an hour, covering the lake with whitecaps. Celebrating the conclusion of a year's hunt, the team decided to make one last trip rather than two and loaded the boat with crocs, gear, and men. Two miles from the mainland the winds worsened and green waves began pouring over the narrow stern of the wooden boat. They quickly jettisoned the crocs, but it was already too late. In seconds the boat filled with water and sank. The trio found themselves adrift in rough seas. Worse yet, the Wildman, who could speak neither English nor Swahili, could not swim a stroke. "His eyes were wide and rolled back, searching Heavenward," remembers Beard.

Alistair quickly disconnected the gas tank and emptied it of fuel so that it would float. Pushing it toward the Wildman, he and Beard spent the next frantic minutes trying to teach him to swim by madly kicking his feet while clutching the tank. The wind was now blowing about thirty miles an hour and the air a foot above the choppy sea was full of spray. Swimming in what they hoped was the right direction, the Wildman and Alistair, who was desperately trying to hang on to his glasses, headed back for Shingle Island.

Beard stayed behind; his diary was in the sunken boat and it contained the crocodile hunt's only records. He found it after four dives into the metal cockpit of the boat, which lay twenty feet under. "For the first time one of my diaries contained something irreplaceable: all of Alistair's croc data, markings, measurements, and tail-scale sequences for age-criteria studies. This made it vital to save," he says.

Beard's swim to Shingle Island was a blur. Clutching his diary he swam against the current and waves. The island, a sandbank the length of a football field, was lying very low in the storm, barely visible above the chop. He tried not to think about the thirty thousand crocodiles that hungered around him.

Eventually he spotted his two friends on shore ahead of him, apparently hugging, slapping, rubbing, and shaking each other. Once out of the water he understood their frantic behavior. The high-octane aviation fuel dumped into the sea had badly burned their skin and the wind on shore

Last photo of "The Curse," September 1966

The march upwind
to assemble a raft for
"Curse" survivors

The raft used for
the two-mile journey to
Shingle Island

immediately brought the resulting pain to their attention.

Assessing the situation—stuck on the island with no one within a hundred miles to miss or rescue them—Beard decided he could make the two-mile swim to the mainland. With the red fuel tank as his float, he set off at 2 P.M. and paddled and kicked for hours to reach shore. The next day, his skin sore and scabbing from gas burns, he rigged a larger float by tying the fuel tank and an empty jerry can together and then flattening another jerry can to serve as a sail. After tieing on emergency rations of Skippy peanut butter and honey, he started his return trip to the tiny island. If he misjudged its position, he risked being blown past it into forty miles of open lake.

He made it after another long swim. Then he and Graham kicked the makeshift craft back to the mainland, and the next day Alistair retrieved his plane, borrowed a boat from Ferguson's Gulf, and went after the Wildman. The survey was indisputably over. By taking just one chance too many they had brought it to an abrupt halt three crocs short of their goal of five hundred. To top it off they had lost their boat, engine, guns, and all other equipment.

More devastating, when the results of their year-long study were written up by Graham and handed over to the Kenyan government, they were promptly filed, never read. Beard reveals this last bit of information gravely. We are readying to leave the lake, and he is saddened by that memory and by what he has seen this past week. The place has changed more in the past twenty-five years than in all the centuries that preceded. The "galloping rot," as he calls the spread of Western-influenced "progress," has even caught up with this most primitive place, and it is daily bespoiled by the march of mankind. Good intentions have delivered the futility of "civilized" man to his birthplace. Fishing nets have reduced the crocodile population to nearly nil.

Driving past the stone-age huts that lead into Kalokol, past women balancing laundry on their heads, past young men in polyester pants and wearing cheap wristwatches, past monstrous cement buildings built and then abandoned, you get the distinct impression that the place and the people were better off before, happy in their primitiveness. "Civilization" has turned them into dependent, handout-oriented beggars. Ironically Graham had predicted this very result, twenty-five years before: "It seems to be the destiny of Walden Ponds, Lake Rudolf included, to be consumed by technological man. And when the wilderness has been sold out, the inevitable remorse."

Flying away from Ferguson's Gulf we buzz low and catch sight of one last reminder of man's insidious intrusion. A mile-long dock sits a mile from the nearest water. It was built in the 1970s by Norad, the Norwegian development agency, and today stretches meaninglessly into the sand. The Norwegians were intent on turning the local Turkana into commercial fishermen, and to encourage them, they built the dock and a $25 million frozen-fish factory. But their plan had deficiencies: The dock's mahogany planks were stolen for firewood days after they were installed, and the frozen-fish factory operated less than a month (the Norwegians had built the monstrosity without considering the enormous amount of diesel fuel that would be required to run a giant air-conditioning unit in the middle of the desert). That debacle is emblematic of how foolish man can be in his attempts to "help."

On the three-hour flight back to Nairobi we stop to refuel in Lodwar. At the airstrip we bump into a pilot friend of Beard's who is flying a borrowed twin-engine jet back from delivering supplies to refugee camps in Sudan. "The greatest irony," Heather Irwin sighs as she explains her mission, "is that starving Ethiopians are now fleeing to Sudan, essentially jumping from the frying pan to the fire." She reports that refugee camps of a hundred thousand and more have erupted along the Sudan side of the Sudanese–Kenyan border.

As we refuel, two dozen small children gather around, introducing us to a new trick. Using fist-sized pieces of foam rubber as sponges, they rush to mop up the gas that overflows during refueling and spills onto the plane's wings. Smiling in anticipation, they jam their fine-boned faces into the gas-soaked foam rubber, sniffing madly, hungrily, for the high.

. . . .

The findings of the Graham/Beard crocodile study did eventually find their way into print. Their book, *Eyelids of Morning: The Mingled Destinies of Crocodile and Men,* was published by the New York Graphic Society in 1972. (During its design, Beard encouraged his growing myth by sleeping in his car in a parking lot on Manhattan's Lower East Side, surrounded by bums and prostitutes "in action atop the hood of my car.")

Like *The End of the Game* the book was well received by critics. Eliot Fremont-Smith wrote in *New York:*

> "It is not that Graham and Beard are against preservation per se; it is that they do not believe true wilderness can exist under civilization's control: the control itself changes things. The tone of their attack on sentimentalists is not designed to win friends and influence Sierra Clubbers—it is often sarcastic and scoldingly imperious. But the substance of the argument, and the real sense of dignity and awe behind it, is worth listening to."

The *Village Voice* wrote, "The authors are sympathetic to our need for mythology, but they waste no time with the sweet ecological lies we live on."

With the book's publication Beard also began to get some personal attention for his unique lifestyle. *Newsweek* dubbed him "bon vivant, photographer, and doomsday chronicler" in a profile that quoted Lee Radziwill ("Many people pretend to be adventurers, but Peter really is") and Richard Avedon ("Every meeting with him or his work knocks me out").

The attention gave Beard a chance to try out some of his newly assimilated theories on wildlife ecology: "Do-gooder conservationists have done the most harm," he told *Newsweek.* "None of them are interested in pictures beyond Joy Adamson French-kissing milk into her lion cub's mouth. The whole emphasis is on one sentimental animal, rather than on the protection of the entire species."

After nearly two years surviving on tins of tuna and warm Fanta, Beard was anxious and ready to jump from the primitive to the gaudy, from Lake Rudolf to Studio 54. The next decade would be packed with highlights, and lowlights, for the increasingly exposed chameleon.

SEVEN

The Diaries: Confessions of a Bookmaker

You know
what they say,
"Little minds
keep big
scrapbooks."

— BEARD

One morning at Lake Rudolf we wake before sunrise, encouraged out of bed by the heat. By 7 A.M. it is already a hundred degrees. Our feet are swollen from stepping on the spear grass that permeates the sand. The flies are so insistent that we roll cans of a potent bug killer, called Doom, back and forth across the linoleum-covered floor as we talk. Though warnings on the cans advise against spraying directly on skin, Beard repeatedly coats his body in the thick poison, badly infecting a deep cut on his leg earned stumbling through the thorn bushes in Tsavo. "I like the rush," he admits. As on most early mornings, Beard is absorbed in his work. Every flat surface around him is piled with newspaper clippings, photographs, feathers, bones, matchbook covers, India ink, and tubes of glue.

The room is thrown wide open—curtains, windows, and door, to the sandy beach. One result is that the Turkana come and go, including Beard's old friend Boiloin and her extended family of brothers, sisters, sons, daughters, and even her sixty-year-old mother.

Beard talks about them while pasting. "These people have absolutely nothing . . . little to eat, no money, few clothes. On the one hand they seem totally desperate. On the other, they seem perfectly happy. By comparison, what have we got? Bills, traffic jams, taxes, all the heartache of materialism, sensory saturation, media glut. . . . It makes you stop and ponder, doesn't it? I know a lot of Park Avenue zillionaires more depressed and ridiculous than these guys."

Sucking on an early-morning beer he is also attempting to talk about his ill-defined "career," even as he works at it. His hands hint at his profession—they are calloused, cut, bruised, and stained, stubby and long at the same time, outsized for the rest of his body. These hands have spent hours ripping apart crocodile armatures and peeling the skin off dik-diks and elephants; they have turned on some of the most beautiful women in

Beard working
on his diary,
Hog Ranch,
1988

the world, hung on to airplane doorframes several thousand feet above the ground in order to get just the right photograph, and picked literally thousands, perhaps millions, of stones and shells off the world's beaches. They are forever ink-stained, lending a hint of Dickens to his character. The ink—black or green, blue, brown, or a deep blood red—is a requirement of his peculiar career. To those he has not met, he introduces himself as a diarist. He insists that to do his diaries justice requires at least an eight-hour day. As well as helping him fill the hours, in many ways the big books he lugs with him everywhere are art, a record of the time. At least his time.

For the past two decades the diaries he has used have been eleven-by-fourteen-inch, red-spined Letts Standard Daily Journals. At year's end the completed recordings offer as close an insight into his enigmatic mind as can be gained. They are crammed with the effluvia of his life: snapshots of friends, newspaper clippings, wildlife pictures, wax drippings, beer bottle labels, frogs, moths, flies, mud, pieces of asphalt, snakeskins, telephone numbers, what he had for dinner, photographs of fashion models, many pictures of Zara and Najma (as well as former wives and girlfriends, including Cheryl Tiegs, Candy Bergen, his first wife, Minnie Cushing, and many, many more), postcards, receipts, feathers, stamps, labels from clothes, phone messages, business cards, contact prints, football line scores, appointments, pen tips, quotes scribbled madly after he's heard them in conversation or on television, used napkins, claim tickets, BBs, records of the time he got up and went to bed, weather reports, menus, Things-To-Do lists, Cheez Doodles, and pressed flowers.

He spits, blows, and bleeds on the pages. In the corner of each, opposite the date, is his location that day: Montauk, New York, Hog Ranch, Nassau, Geneva, and elsewhere. Inside the cover of 1991's diary are pasted two words clipped from newspaper headlines: "Lucky" and "Censored."

"These books are not comparable to anything else in the whole natural world," claimed one New York critic after seeing the books on display. "They fall somewhere between the organic and inorganic, between vegetable and mineral." Joe Helman, who owns Blum Helman, the Manhattan gallery that represents Beard, has called the books "the most important chronicle of these times."

"I just hope for really good accidents," says Beard. He does not search for accolades for what he regards as very personal books-in-progress. "Little by little, at the end of the year I have an enormous life-thickening thing, like an organic accordion. It's completely ludicrous, messy, and futile, but it's there. The books have something to them, but I don't really know what yet. It's funny that the two things I love most—collecting stones and doing diaries—are equally meaningless."

Polaroid studio,
1989

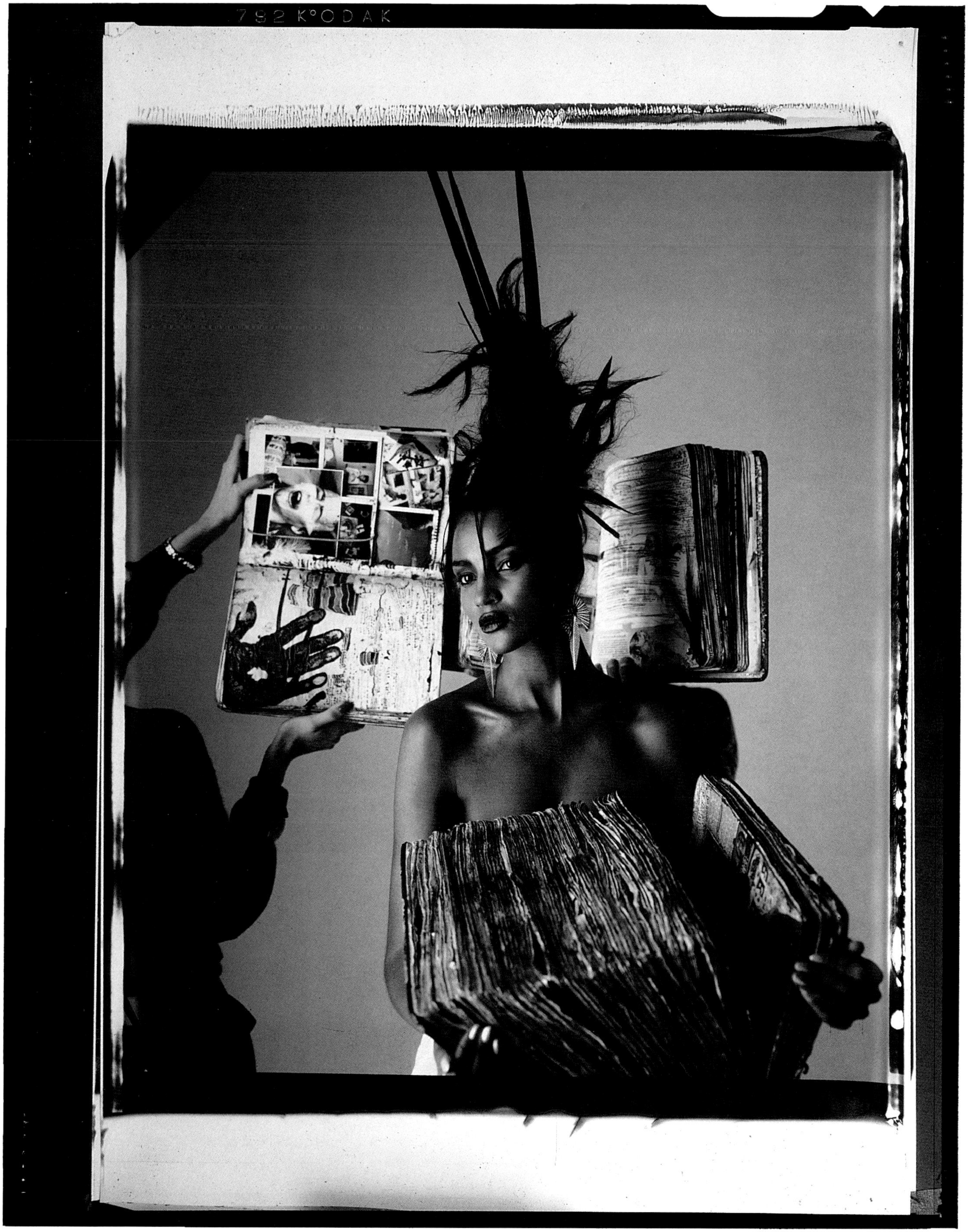
782 KODAK

up @ 8:45 ... Diary
9am Brakfers APRIL
Bob ...A8 & co off to NBI ... Miles Air Strip

PHOTOS in eaten out BAOBAB
HUGH and CRY
getting that ele back together again
as evidenced by the persistant track ?!
Mzima Syrings horror show of Vervets + tourists ...
one for the Road ... return Hog Ranch via Chulus ...
Richard + Iain car stuck on Bananna Hill ...
Dinner of T. Soup and Tuna + Beeley
Ethiopia Natl. park is created
and Smallpox gets on the Endangered species list ...

MAY
TAVETA – RAIN

Tuesday apr. 19 MONTAUK
a vivdure nostrum day (1st humm...)
after voyage – O. Vallen over w/fra
for MARY HARTMAN ... jumped fnd + N.G
EVAN Calls fr. Nairobi all wt...
Maggie back late today fr. Santa Domingo
cable R.B. ... Pro Cam. Rep LENSE LOST
(Ele. lense – E.K lense) #####

'Human Bomb'
Jailed in Britain

TEESIDE, England, April 13
(UPI) — Gibbon Hedley, 48, a
jilted husband who turned himself into a human bomb, was
jailed for five years yesterday for
killing his wife's lover.
The court heard that Hedley
decided to kill Wilfred Rutherford, 54, when he discovered Mr.
Rutherford was having an affair
with his wife (Sheila, 39. Hedley
stuffed explosives under his coat,
hung a detonator around his
neck and hunted Mr. Rutherford
down. When he found him,
Hedley pressed the button.
There was a shattering explosion, but both men emerged alive.
Hedley staggered over to his
wounded victim and battered him
to death with the detonator box,
the court was told.

COMMAND YOUR FOLLOWERS
TO RELEASE ALL PRISONERS!
I – I'M COMPELLED TO
OBEY-GUARDS, RE-
LEASE YOUR CAPTIVES!

KLIP
Pepsi +

Bosky off @ 12:
"seen any Lion?"

MONTAUK

saturday hot 80°
Stevens Chicken Lunch dinner
@ 7:8 pm ... Dennis + Julie

**'MALICIOUS RUMOURS
MUST END' WARNING**
PEOPLE must stop spreading
malicious rumours aimed at
disrupting peace and stability in the
country...

4 3

$3.50

Four-page collage
by Peter Beard
for *Rolling Stone*
yearbook,
1990

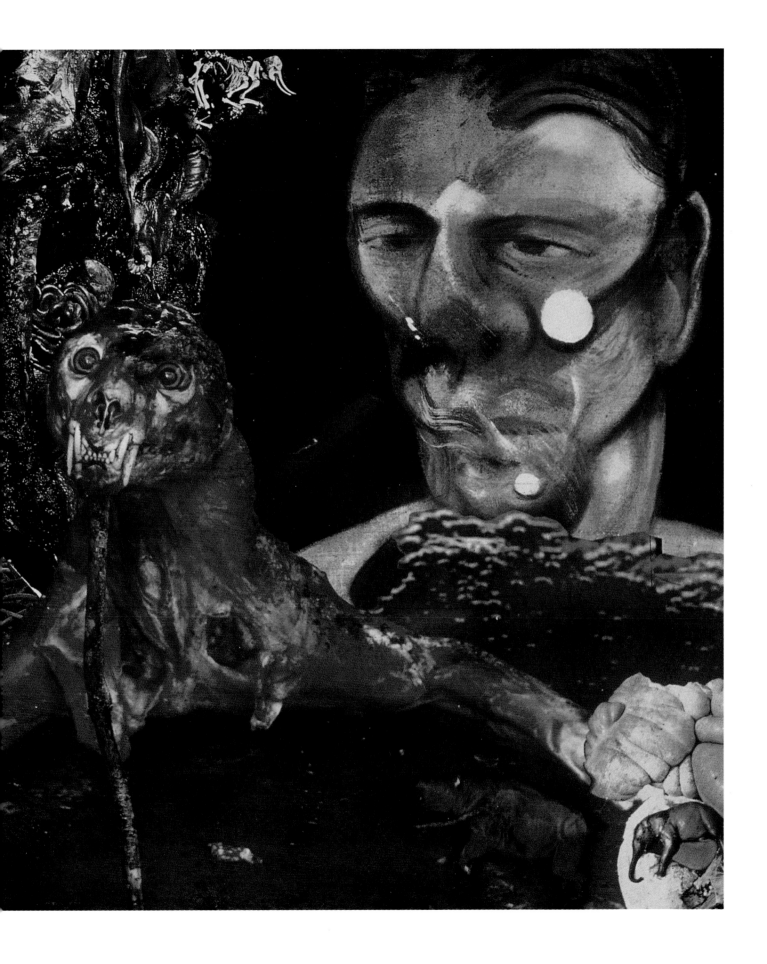

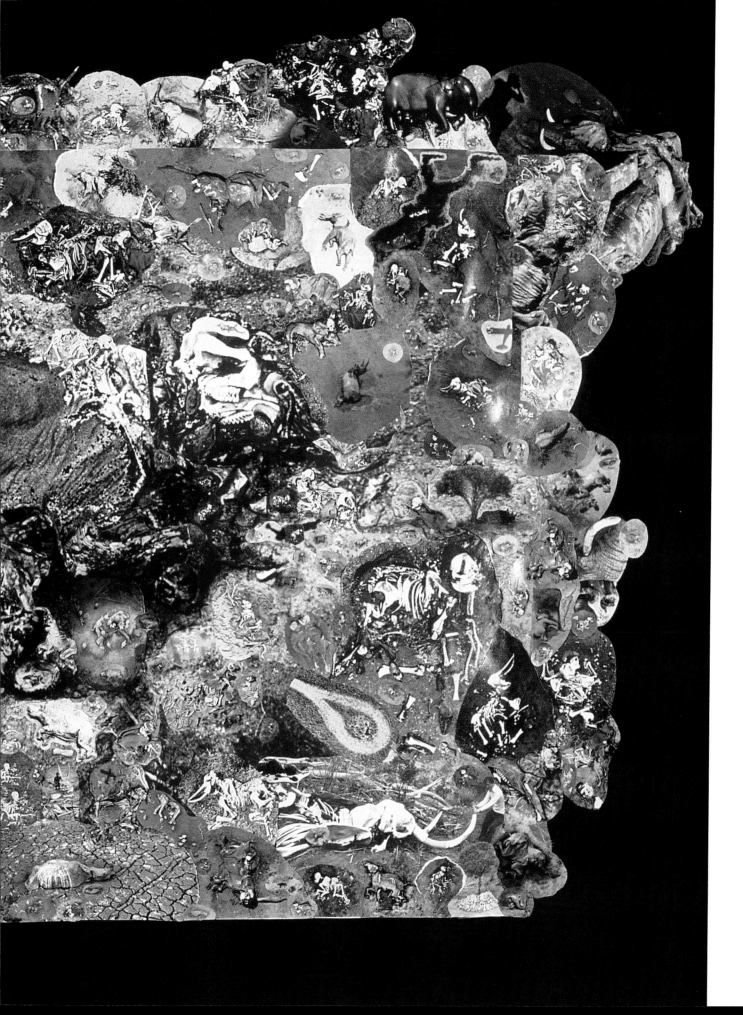

Diaries and images
rephotographed by Beard
in Montauk,
1992–93

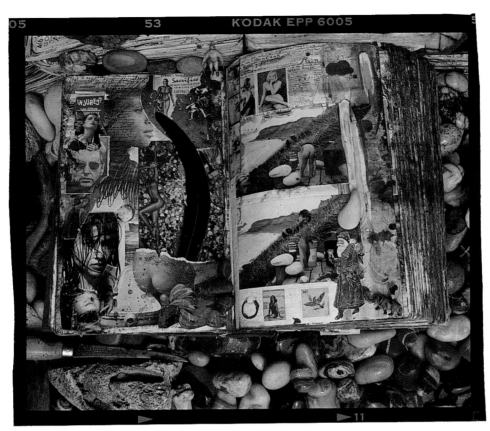

Diary
with Zara's
hand

His first diary was kept in 1949. Encouraged by his "nagging" mother, Beard made the little book while on vacation, cramming it with seashells, clumps of hair, horses' tails, and bottle caps. At Yale he drew in the margins of textbooks, soon making them illegible, so he began putting his jottings and "stuff" into a book of their own.

Each year's diary has been individual. The one combining the years 1959 through 1961 has some photographs and a lot of very straight drawings—very detailed portraits in old-master techniques. The biggest ever was a huge, loose-leaf affair covering 1963 to 1965. At that point the diaries "stopped being diaries and became just a place where I could put extra things." The first devoted solely to Africa (in 1963–64) was very small, filled with tiny writing. Another kept over the same period, 1963–65, was crammed with more than two thousand photographs and grew to seven inches thick. In 1967–68 Beard kept his diaries on yellow legal pads; in 1969 he turned to the big red and brown Letts Journals he uses still.

Year by year the diaries grew more complex. Beard reveled in them because they were something he could work on as long as he wanted without fearing they would ever reach the end. What distinguished them was their ability to incorporate things—newspaper headlines, photos, tidbits of life—from disparate worlds and mold them into one. While each element was borrowed from extreme and alien places, the entire assemblage was original. Each page became imbued with Beard's own tone, sensibility, and what he calls "debonaire morbidity," no matter the origins of the ingredients. Not ironically, the same tendency—to borrow ideas, theories, and gossip from those around him and make them his own—is evident in his speech, his books, and the whole character of his often dark mind.

Though the diaries tell where he went, with whom, how the weather was, and what he had for dinner, you won't find out from reading them who their maker really is. Beard rarely offers glimpses into his own formative experiences or emotional life. Somehow, though, the diaries are exceedingly personal, evocative records of his days. While many think of him as just a photographer, he is more a multivisioned artist. Like Andy Warhol or Alexander Calder, Beard turns everything he touches into some kind of art. The Steadmanesque drawings and list makings that crowd the diaries, usually done in the wee hours of the night on into the early morning, are indicators of a haunted, visionary mind that rarely rests. Some days he works on the books from sunup to long past midnight. Other days he skips them altogether. He admits that they are an addiction. He calls himself today "a slave to trivia."

"They have many meanings for me," Beard says of his diaries, spraying a long flume of Doom down his back. "In college I started them to prevent boredom. Mainly they record the gory details and extremes in life on the same and opposite pages. This is really the outsider's drive in life—to sort out the extreme situations and emotions so that in the middle you have some delicate dynamic harmonies and moments of fleeting understanding of both sides at once. Those are the magic moments."

Beard's aesthetic accidents fascinate critics of both art and society-at-large. Filmmaker Jonas Mekas has labeled them "grotesque graveyards of the Western Civilization." "Peter is obsessed with recording what is gone, what's not here," Mekas wrote in the *Soho News*. "He takes his materials from the huge garbage heap of Western Civilization. With his glue and

his scissors he sits among it all, very, very happy. I don't think he keeps it to remember it. I don't think he's doing it for any reason, purpose or goal. He just does it, like some insects or worms do, collecting the crumbs of civilization into huge anthills of books and diaries."

Photo critic Owen Edwards sees the diaries as a "combination of adolescent daydreaming, fiendish detritus, cosmic dandruff, frantic tangible psychotherapy and visual novas page after exhausting page.

"Like Beard, his uncommon commonplace books are hard to describe in anything less than a chapter loaded with Freudian asides and sniffed-out demon's trails," Edwards wrote in *The Village Voice.* "I suspect they are a safety valve to bleed off steam from a perpetually overheated mind. The recorded ravings, mumbles and psychic tics of a manifestly singular character, they are ultimately too personal to be of more than a parochial interest." Beard claims that Warhol started keeping diaries after he saw his. "Andy once asked me why my writing was so small. Because life is so small, I guess. Eighty years means nothing. Smallness makes more room for a lot of trivia."

Over the years the diaries have involved Beard in a couple of scrapes, particularly on a trip to Nicaragua where the customs folks were extremely interested in the big book he carried under his arm. He panicked as they paged through it, thinking that they would focus on the pictures of naked women and trump up some kind of "obscene materials" charge.

The most revelatory experience occurred after the sinking of "The Curse" in Lake Rudolf. When he and Graham returned to Shingle Island to pick up the Wildman, Beard hurried to see what had happened to his diary after its dunking. Miraculously, none of the pages was wet, thanks to the stranded native, who had turned every page until it dried out beneath the sun. Though the ink had run and bled, though bits of seaweed and sand were now mixed in, Beard took one look at the bulging, weather-beaten book and was overjoyed.

"The ink-embedded photos never looked so good," he wrote. "Nine months of hoarded scraps had fossilized themselves. Before my eyes the unrelated pieces merged in monster mildewed unities of trivial pursuit, all bursting forth in clouds of spill and drip, exploding blossoms, blowing in the wind. Great soak-through seepings turned from mediocre mess to magic, the wondrous workings of pure accident."

Ever since, he has encouraged any and all accidents in his books.

I ask Beard if his diaries are more than personal. Does he, for example, consider them art?

"Who cares?" he barks, in the tone reserved for questions he regards as utterly ridiculous. "Personal is already enough. It's just an involvement for myself. Everyone looks at the things differently. Take this, for example. I had a show in Japan and this guy came up to me and said, 'This is really embarrassing.' I said, 'Great.' But he was serious. He said, 'I'm from America and this is one of the most embarrassing things I've ever seen.' I didn't know what he was getting at, but I understood. Human activity *is* embarrassing. One gets a lot of insights, not directly but indirectly, from doing these commonplace books."

He relishes sharing the diaries. The Turkana have brought him snakeskins this morning, which he encourages them to drop into the pages wherever they choose. "When people say they like something about them, that entertains me greatly. Look, I appreciate any echo, okay, but I almost prefer showing them to these people [the Turkana] because they look at them openly, differently, and have no idea what they mean . . . and I'm not sure anyone should—even me. I know when a page comes into its own; only forty or fifty a year ever work. A Japanese company is making wallpaper out of some of the best pages, and it will be fun to see them all together."

Each year Beard attempts to stretch the medium. For example, he's considering using 1991's diary for 1992 as well, thus layering two years' experiences on the same pages. One hope he has is to someday publish a book of many thousands of pages drawn from his years of diaries. He already knows the book's title: *From a Dead Man's Wallet.* "I once saw an airplane crash in Connecticut, in which eleven people were killed. Every one of them was thrown out of their tightly tied shoes . . . and I saw a lot of wallets strewn around. Looking inside the plane was the strangest experience, lots of insight."

His passion for diary making may sound like a trivial pursuit to some, but one thing you have to understand about Beard is his childlike ability to be absorbed in the moment. He is intensely fascinated with whatever is on his plate at that very instant, so what might seem boring to others—like pasting together diaries for eight, ten hours a day—is fascinating to him. The same intensity applies whether he's reading the daily papers or single-mindedly stalking a rhino with a camera deep in the Greater Shag.

"Let's face it, the diaries are an exercise in futility," he readily admits. "That's what art is. Oscar Wilde said it best: 'Art is everything useless.' I agree."

EIGHT

· · · · · · · · · · ·

First Trouble

Shortly after leaving Lake Rudolf in 1966 Beard fell deeply, madly, and, according to his friends, permanently in love. ("Hardly," contends Beard when I ask.) It wasn't the first time he'd introduced a beautiful woman to the bush, but this was different, truly a storybook romance.

Mary O. "Minnie" Cushing, the daughter of Howard Gardiner Cushing, was from one of Newport's oldest families. She and Beard had met briefly in 1965 at the New Stanley Hotel; she returned several months later, and they became inseparable.

"They are like Tarzan and Jane," said Carol Bell, a friend of both at the time. "He's strong and brave, she's beautiful. They're both beautiful." Minnie was dubbed "society's girl of the year," by one magazine, with "fashion model dimensions" and "traffic-stopping loveliness." They were married on August 12, 1967, before 416 guests in Newport's historic Trinity Church. A police motorcade escorted them to the church, and after the reception they were flown from the Cushings' seaside estate by helicopter. The wedding was judged one of America's social highlights of the year.

The couple's first year of marriage was spent mostly together at Hog Ranch and in the bush, traveling between the Aberdares, Lake Rudolf, and Ukambani. Hog Ranch became a second home to the Newport crowd. Minnie labeled their early days in Kenya together "magical," but it was a hard life. Beard was looking for a companion ready to go as far as he would and was hard-pressed to countenance weakness or whimpering (even when Minnie was bitten by a snake). In the summer of 1968 she returned home to visit her mother and never returned to Africa. "She got tired of playing Maureen O'Sullivan to his Johnny Weissmuller," said a friend.

"There were times I almost felt I was losing a personality, but really it was blossoming," Minnie would tell a reporter years later. "I'm still very earmarked. I still have a lot from him." As for Beard, he admired her then as now. "She is the greatest. Always was. But ultimately her 'love' for Africa turned out to be just an act."

ABOVE

· · · · · · · · ·

Minnie
with General Kifaru,
a Mau Mau leader

RIGHT

· · · · · · · · · · · ·

Minnie
with Northi-chongo
(a one-eyed vervet monkey),
Hog Ranch,
1968

Kenyan-born Carol Bell, later to become another of Beard's girlfriends, intimates that Beard was changed forever by Minnie. "Peter loved the bush and lived in it the way the Africans did, without tents or even sleeping bags. He could go for weeks and months into the bush. That changed after marrying Minnie. She tried, but couldn't live like that. She got sick, and Peter had no patience for such 'weakness.' Still, the breakup with Minnie really hurt him—and he never really went back to the bush. The society side of his life had won him back."

Hard-hit by Minnie's disappearing act, Beard followed her back to the States, where they took up residence in a small apartment on West Fifty-seventh Street. But she got involved with the producer of Broadway's *Hair* and was granted a quickie divorce in Mexico. Beard and Minnie were married just two years, but even when he talks about her today you sense she was his first real love and perhaps his greatest loss. Photographs of her are still pinned up all over the Hog Ranch studio and scattered throughout his diaries.

The breakup with Minnie culminated in Beard's near demise, a first indicator to some of a darker side to the seemingly always buoyant raconteur. On January 18, 1969, as he told *Rolling Stone,* "I was really wrecked at the time and so short on sleep I just super od-ed, and was heading for the ultimate relaxation, copping my final zees so to speak, but still conscious and pretty happy about the whole thing as a matter of fact when, in one of those one in a million accidents, a friend called at this absurd hour of the morning and woke me up."

He'd nearly swallowed one barbiturate too many and didn't wake up until his birthday, four days later, in New York Hospital. Concerned that he was suicidal, doctors advised his parents to admit him to Payne Whitney Psychiatric Ward. He spent five months there.

"Basically I had lost interest in everything," he remembers today. "Then I wasted weeks talking to psychoanalysts about my stressed world."

· · · · · · · · · ·

Beard and I are sitting at a corner table at the Thorn Tree Café, watching the tourists and the prostitutes gambol. He is trying to explain this blurb I'd come across in a 1969 issue of *Time:* "Among his friends in Kenya, Beard was considered to be a brilliant American eccentric, a millionaire's son dressed most of the time like a hobo. For the crime of assaulting a Kenyan farmhand suspected of poaching, he faces eighteen months behind bars, and twelve strokes with a cane on his bare buttocks."

"We didn't know who it was at first," he begins, as a way of explaining the April 1968 assault. "We were clearing bush at Hog Ranch and kept running across snares, nearly forty in all. So Galo-Galo staked out the area and waited for the poacher to come back. That was after we found a trapped suni, a very rare, rabbit-sized antelope, in one of the snares.

"Galo-Galo watched the guy come and retrieve the suni from the snare. He knew right where it was, walked straight to it. He was a Mkamba, carrying a *panga* [machete] and a *rungu* [club]. When Galo-Galo confronted him, he got quite aggressive and claimed he'd happened on the snare by accident. Galo-Galo let him go on his way, then came and got me.

"We went next door, to Mervyn Cowie's, where this guy worked. Cowie was the founder of the national parks! The Mkamba still claimed he was innocent, but I asked him to show us where he'd been walking. It was obvious he was lying. We got to the site and I said, 'Okay, now show me where the rest of your snares are hidden, or you're going to stay here in this one!' He continued to deny he knew anything about them . . . waffling like mad.

"So I hit him, once, as hard as I could, to sort of bring him back to reality. But I might as well have been hitting a rock, it had hardly any effect on him. Since the blow didn't achieve its objective, we put him in the snare and gagged him with a glove. I photographed the suni and the guy in the snare and then went off to have the films developed—and have lunch. Galo-Galo stayed behind to watch the scene. I'd told him we'd let him go when he was ready to tell us where the rest of his snares were hidden.

"Any other story you hear is *fitina* [gossip], and there are a million versions: that I tortured him, strung him up between two trees 'in a dangerous part of the forest'—that's what the local papers wrote. In fact, he was in the snare for an hour and a half. I went into town, had the films developed, had lunch and came back. By then it had started to rain and Galo-Galo had undone him and returned to camp. My Africans had let him out."

Eighteen months later, in November 1969, police from Karen came to Hog Ranch and arrested Beard and Galo-Galo on charges of assault and wrongful confinement. After a five-day trial, both were found guilty on both charges. Beard was sentenced to nine months imprisonment and twelve strokes on the first charge, and nine months on the second, with prison sentences to run consecutively; Galo-Galo's sentence was six strokes and three months on each charge. Before they could cry foul, they were whisked into a holding pen with eighteen other felons. Beard's head was shaved, he was assigned number 41632, and carted off to Kamiti, Kenya's meanest and filthiest prison. "The sentence shook everyone," he says today.

Kamante, suni,
and Galo-Galo Guyu,
who caught the
poacher

Beard (out on bail)
stranded on Central Island,
Lake Rudolf,
1969

41632

JIO.
+
POT

Beard spent ten days in Kamiti. Lights were out at 4:30 P.M.; rise and shine was at 5 A.M. He slept on the cold cement floor, next to "a thousand other guys." "It was especially hard going to the loo," he says, "it was so revolting some guys tried not to eat or drink, so they wouldn't have to go." One of his cellmates was a white policeman in on a trumped-up charge of "being seen on the same bed as an African," a thinly masked charge of homosexual behavior.

Ruth Woodley remembers visiting Beard in jail. "Our mutual friend Jack Block, whose family owned the New Stanley Hotel, the Norfolk, and others in Kenya, tried to get me to go to court and say he [Beard] was mentally incapable of standing trial. I wasn't about to go on record with such a lie. When I visited him in jail, he had a big smile on his face." Beard's girlfriend at the time, Carol Bell, remembers him as being somewhat oblivious to the severity of his confinement. "Whenever Peter got in trouble he thought it was no big deal, just another 'experience,'" she says.

Ten days after being jailed Beard was out on $2,500 bail put up by Block, who had also quietly appealed to J. M. Kariuki, a friend of President Jomo Kenyatta's, to see if some presidential persuasion might be granted on the American's behalf. Across the Atlantic appeals were already being made by the State Department at the urging of Beard's friend Jackie Onassis. There were rumors that the Kenyan government wanted Beard deported.

A review of the case was granted quickly, in part due to growing international pressure. The judge this time was more lenient, and on January 8, 1970, gave both Beard and Galo-Galo conditional discharges on the first count and ordered the prison sentences imposed on the second set aside. Beard was fined five hundred pounds and Galo-Galo, twenty-five pounds—half of each went to the poacher. After announcing that the prison sentences would be dropped, the judge cautioned that their "justifiable determination to bring the poacher to justice was taken too far." Insiders implied that an arrest never would have been made had Beard gone straight to the police with his complaint rather than to lunch. It was apparently the insouciant attitude of the American that angered the police more than the act itself. Beard says it was simply racism.

When Beard and Galo-Galo left the courtroom they were greeted roundly by a gathering of African friends. The lasting effect of the incident on his reputation has been mixed. The assault charge made him seem more dangerous than he probably was (though an unpredictable temper has long been part of his personality), and still today among Africans in Langata and Ongata Rongai, he is known as "The Hangman." He says it is that reputation that has kept Hog Ranch free from bandits over the years.

Beard
out on bail from
Kamiti Prison,
1969

NINE

Kurt Vonnegut told me once that when he witnessed 30,000 people die at Dresden he felt as if he owned the whole horror, that the weight was on his shoulders. That was the way I felt about Tsavo.

— BEARD

Tsavo II: Dead Elephants

Although I'd heard the words Ecology and Environment before, although I'd been to the dark continent several times in the Fifties, I only ended up in the conservation field by accident, by total chance, by process of elimination. As a result I very casually observed what has to be described as the very opposite of conservation.

— BEARD

The Yatta Plateau, a great tongue of lava (the longest such flow in the world) rises like a rampart from the rivers and dry plains along the western edge of Tsavo. One late afternoon we drove up and over the plateau, Beard and I standing in the bed of a Land Cruiser pickup. He was madly, and inexplicably, singing a medley of Christmas songs (Najma, who was riding in the cab, assured me that that meant he was happy). Having spent the day climbing the steep face of the Yatta, we were headed for the Athi River, which tumbled below lined by doum palms. We'd been in the bush for a week and were anxious for a cold beer and hot shower.

Half the day had been spent on our knees crawling through thick *nyika* (thorn bushes), under acacias connected with a network of creepers and draped with masses of convolvulus. "Wait-a-bit" thorns ripped at our clothing and skin. A pair of young, smooth-skinned rangers, armed with automatic rifles, accompanied us. We saw tracks of beast and man, most likely Somali or Kamba poachers.

In the sandy bed of the dry river that paralleled the plateau we ran across footprints of giraffes and dik-diks, and elephant and buffalo spoor, but spotted none of the animals who left them. Then Beard, who has retained his incredible "game eyes," glimpsed a lioness a hundred yards ahead, lazing in the heated sand and facing downriver, away from us. We crouched down as quietly as possible as she monitored the area, ratcheting her head nearly 360 degrees until she caught us in her high-powered sight. With two bounds, she was off into the bush.

Beard
and an elephant
from the confines of
overcrowded
Amboseli population

Back in the Land Cruiser we climbed a dirt track that rose up the plateau, the top of which was as flat as a football field. As we raced along, Danny Woodley at the wheel, a half dozen fifteen-foot-tall giraffes galloped alongside. A rare Marshall eagle sat in a young baobab tree watching our progress. Beard pointed out each baobab, since there are just a few still standing in Tsavo. Known as "The Tree Where Man Was Born," baobabs are the only large tree to live in this *nyika* and are said to grow for a thousand years. They are home to nesting eagles, red-billed buffalo weavers, owls, bats, bushbabies, and, many Africans believe, ghosts. The Kamba tribesmen call the tree "a house of spirits" and suggest its weird "upside-down" appearance was its punishment for not growing where God wanted it to. Swahili legend claims the devil himself upturned the trees in a rage, daring them to survive the indignity of his leaving their roots exposed. Twenty years ago thousands of the rotund, scarred trees graced Tsavo. Today seeing one intact is a comparative rarity, since most were destroyed by starving elephants in the early 1970s. The lack of baobabs is just one sign of the devastation that wracked the park. The thick bush atop the Yatta Plateau is another: If the elephant population had come back to any degree it would have browsed through this bush, clearing paths as it progressed; the impenetrable, thick bush is evidence that few beasts are spending time here.

As it turned out, Dick Laws was right in 1966. The drought he had predicted came, and the elephant population—much too large for the park to sustain, especially during a drought—died in large numbers from malnutrition, heart disease, and constipation. Starving elephants ate the baobabs, pushing them over to get at the leaves and branches, and gouging the trunks for edible fiber. They left a blitzed, battle-scarred plain in their wake. Between nine thousand (David Sheldrick's figure) and forty thousand (Murray Watson's figure) elephants died in and around Tsavo. The result of letting nature take its course was that ten times the elephants died that would have if the culling Laws had recommended had taken place.

Perhaps Beard's most important single photograph is one of the boundary line at Tsavo taken in 1975. The land outside the park is thick and green, while the land inside looks like a T. S. Eliot wasteland, just desertlike soil and a thin scattering of mostly dead shrubs and trees.

The Tsavo of today—vast but vacant of animals—is the result of a confluence of factors: the vagaries of climate, including a major drought, and an increase in poachers, both Somali and Kenyan. Most important, however, is the controversial debate over exactly how wildlife and parkland should be managed. It is a centuries-old concern: what to do once man has moved into a wilderness area. The destruction that ruined Tsavo is one of the planet's best examples of what can happen as man debates. While

Tsavo warden David Sheldrick within half-eaten baobab tree, Tsavo East, 1964

fingers have been pointed in every direction these past twenty years, the bottom line is that something failed at Tsavo in spite of the best intentions.

If it hadn't been for the growth in Kenya's human population, Tsavo's elephants could have moved on at any time, as they had for centuries before when droughts occurred, to other, more fertile sections of Kenya. But in 1970, if they stepped outside the park's borders, they risked harassment by farmers, Somali poachers, and native Kenyan hunters. Nor was the management of Tsavo helped by the fact that for many years the parks were run by an inefficient, largely unqualified board of trustees. What the parks needed was professional management, by educated staffs that included trained ecologists. The lesson learned at Tsavo is that the wild is not a controlled laboratory; what works in theory does not necessarily work in practice. As Beard points out, "The parks are man-made and they have to be man-managed."

The Tsavo die-off began two years after Dick Laws and his team of scientists were kicked out of the park. Beard, who was privy to all sides of the debate, remembers those years distinctly. "While the management debate raged," he says, "elephants continued to destroy the woodland over much of the two parks [Tsavo East and West], leaving behind acres of dead and battered wood. The elephants in Tsavo ate—and destroyed—a national park bigger than Israel or Massachusetts and then starved to death in the desert they created at our hands." By 1970 the elephants had exceeded Tsavo's carrying capacity and were eating their food supply to the bottom of the dust bowl. The baobabs fell over and crushed them to death as they gnawed on the trunks. What was once a forest floor became an open graveyard littered with carcasses. For several years after, Tsavo resembled a virtual desert.

The flattened forest was an open invitation to ivory poachers who could simply drive in, pull the tusks from the rotting carcasses, and drive away unchallenged. The natives, their crops failing due to the drought, also took to the bush to retrieve the tusks of dead elephants. "Word of the 'ivory-mine' traveled fast and far, and soon the parks were filled with Somalis, Kamba and more," writes Ian Parker in *Ivory Crisis,* "and the parks couldn't stop them. As the supply of ivory from the die-off dwindled, the ivory searchers took to hunting. Unimpeded by bush, the poachers were able to drop herds in great numbers, much as we had done in Murchison. By 1974 the number of elephants dying from the attention of the poachers far exceeded those dying of malnutrition and worse." The die-off swept through a vast area: from Lugards Falls and Aruba Dam, then up and down the Yatta Plateau, across the Tiva River to Ithumba all the way to Daka Dema and beyond. Yet even while it was happening, it was being denied in Kenya by park administrators.

The Tsavo border
in 1975.
The park, ravaged by
starving elephants,
is on the left.
The hunting block is
on the right.

By the early 1970s corruption had infiltrated all strata of Kenya's government, and it was widely known that some of the biggest poached-ivory dealers in Africa were relatives of Kenya's president at the time, Jomo Kenyatta. Government officials were the biggest beneficiaries of illegal ivory smuggling. It was no secret that the head of the Wildlife Conservation and Management Division of the Ministry of Tourism and Wildlife was one of the country's strongest defenders of poachers—because he received kickbacks from them.

Beard is explaining Tsavo's recent history as we start down the back side of the Yatta. Along the Athi we stop at Tsavo Safaris, the tent-camp Beard had helped Glen Cottar build in the early 1960s. Beard, Bill Woodley, and I head for the bar to quench dusty throats. The place is filled with memories for both men, some good, some bad.

Bill Woodley knows Tsavo better than any man alive. "One reason there are so few ellies today is because we can shoot Somalis, but we can't shoot our own rangers," he notes with irony. According to Woodley, who worked for the parks for forty-three years, Sheldrick's park rangers were in on the hunt as well, shooting elephants for their increasingly valuable tusks. Rhinos were not excepted from the slaughter. Between four thousand and five thousand died in the 1970s, mostly from starvation but quite a few from the effects of .303 bullets fired from the rifles of the anti-poaching patrols. By 1978, nearly 50 percent of the poaching cases reported in Kenya involved members of the Ministry of Wildlife and Tourism.

. . . .

It is the pictures of the destruction of Tsavo, the photographs of dying elephants, "spinning madly in the dirt . . . screwing themselves maniacally into the dust for days and weeks until they finally died from starvation," that are the most powerful of Beard's career in Africa.

He took his camera into the park in the 1970s against the wishes of his old mentor/tormentor Sheldrick, photographing the destruction primarily from an airplane flying several hundred feet above the ground. "You could smell the rotting carcasses from two thousand feet. Some were still dying," he says. The hauntingly detached and weirdly abstract pictures he shot—dubbed by one critic "hieroglyphs of doom"—were to become his signature images. "Rotting, disappearing carcasses are the best possible subject matter because everything's happening so freely and spontaneously and incredibly abstractly," he says today. "Each dynamic sculpture fell apart differently, with anguish and humor, oozing with imagery."

He sneaked into the park aided by his old Wildlife Services pals Richard Bell, Ian Parker, and Murray Watson—based out of the Ngulia Safari Lodge in Tsavo West—who piloted him usually at altitudes far below the twenty-

five hundred feet that was law. Sheldrick and his rangers tried desperately to catch them. As a ruse, Beard would have someone else—usually Parker or Bell—drive his clearly marked Land Cruiser into the park, drawing the attention of the park's rangers and diverting attention from his low-flying plane. Once he went so far as to borrow a red wig from an American friend, Tish Hewitt, and drive into the park unnoticed. He would have messages delivered to Sheldrick that said, "I'm at Cottar's Camp, wish you were here."

Meanwhile, Sheldrick and his rangers were scurrying to defuse the impact of the dead and dying elephants. "David would locate the carcasses, then fly over them in tight turns," says Beard. "Then his rangers would run miles and miles overland to retrieve the ivory. They hacked the tusks out to make it appear the animals had been poached, not starved to death. On other occasions Murray Watson claimed Sheldrick had a mental block when it came to seeing the dead elephants . . . he'd fly over them and blank them out."

Beard insists that the Tsavo tragedy and subsequent controversy led to Sheldrick's death. Watson's estimate that between thirty thousand and forty thousand elephants had died in and around Tsavo weighed heavily on Kenya's senior warden. Soon after the last ellie starved, Sheldrick was "promoted" to a desk job in Nairobi. He died in 1978. "Thankfully for him he never saw my dead elephant pictures," says Beard. "Seeing them would have probably killed him."

Sheldrick defended his no-culling decision until his death. In the mid-1970s, in *Africana* magazine, he wrote: "In Tsavo . . . the policy is to encourage the natural emergence of a diverse habitat capable of supporting undisturbed the greatest variety of animals in the largest possible numbers, and as this is the goal towards which we must strive, we can be confident that the indications so far that we are on the right road. . . . Only the lack of rain, and the subsequent absence of vegetational regrowth coupled with the low protein content of the available browse caused the death of the elephant and rhino in the drought of 1970–71 . . . it came as no surprise, and, indeed, was considered a necessary process of nature in the best long-term interest of the Park. . . ."

* * * * * * * * * *

Beard amassed thousands of photographs of thousands of dead and dying elephants. Owen Edwards calls that body of work "one of the most extraordinary collections of images ever produced." Beautiful and ghastly in varying degrees, the elephants lie dead in ironically lifelike running positions, their bodies like random stains on the barren ground. The photographs are at once real and unearthly, in a way rare even for the eccentric

Flight
over Tsavo,
1971

123

capacities of photography. Beard's elephants, vultured and rotting, are not just unprecedented views of the end of an epoch, they are intimations of the end of the world.

"You can never plan pictures like that," says Beard. It's another day along the crocodile-infested Athi River and after a long walk we've taken riverside seats on stumps. "Everything was happening quickly. Isn't that the whole point of photography, to get those things you can't repeat?

"In many ways I was just lucky . . . like Hemingway was lucky in the places he chose to visit. He had an incredible genius for finding the right place at the right time, including Key West, Cuba, and Kenya in the 1930s. Paradises, each of them.

"My luck was finding a subject matter that intrigued me. I came to Africa selfishly, to get away from it all and get into the wildlife scene, the 'primitava.' It turned out, by sheer luck, to be much better than I could have planned. Everywhere I went, things seemed to die and decay. Even people—Philip Percival, J. A. Hunter, Grogan, Karen Blixen—everybody I met and photographed seemed to fade away soon afterwards. It sounds odd, but I was extremely fortunate. Most of the dead ellie pictures were taken in a matter of weeks."

124

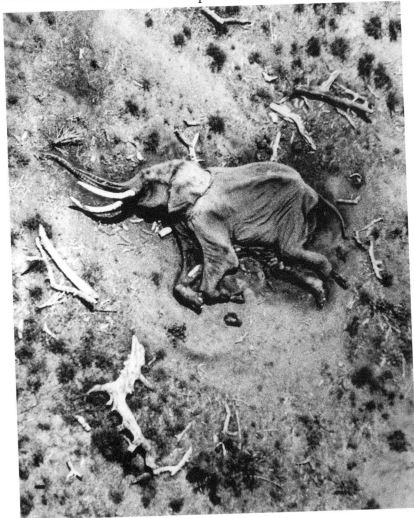

Dead elephant
with ivory firmly
in place,
1972

Ironically, many more of those pictures were lost. "After two weeks of shooting from the air I had seventy rolls of just dead elephants, a body a click so to speak. I put them all in a *wocamba* [woven] basket and returned to Hog Ranch.

"When I got home a bottle of brandy was missing. I'd never missed any alcohol before so it boiled down to the new night watchman. I confronted him, and told him the next time it happened he'd be gone. He was extremely uptight and the next morning he was doing his menial tasks with extra energy and cleaned out all the wastebaskets in camp, including the one full of all the unexposed films. He threw them all into the fire . . . I was able to rake five rolls out of the fire, but saved only two or three pictures." What was lost? Beard replies in world-weary voice, "Probably the greatest pictures I ever took."

By the mid-seventies, despite his growing portfolio and fast-expanding international reputation, Beard was growing increasingly disillusioned with his paradise. He had developed a truly grassroots understanding of the problems facing Kenya's wildlife scene and was not hesitant to voice his opinions. The "galloping rot" of civilization he'd hoped to escape was now blanketing even Africa. It was no longer the roadless, mapless place of the Blixen era, but was becoming a fenced and partitioned refuge for humans. In Beard's mind it was growing increasingly ugly. "In America the ugliness is imposed on suburbia; in Africa it's imposed on paradise. It's much more painful to watch.

"My biggest disappointment (in Tsavo) was that incredibly expensive experts were hired to analyze the situation professionally. They reported,

125

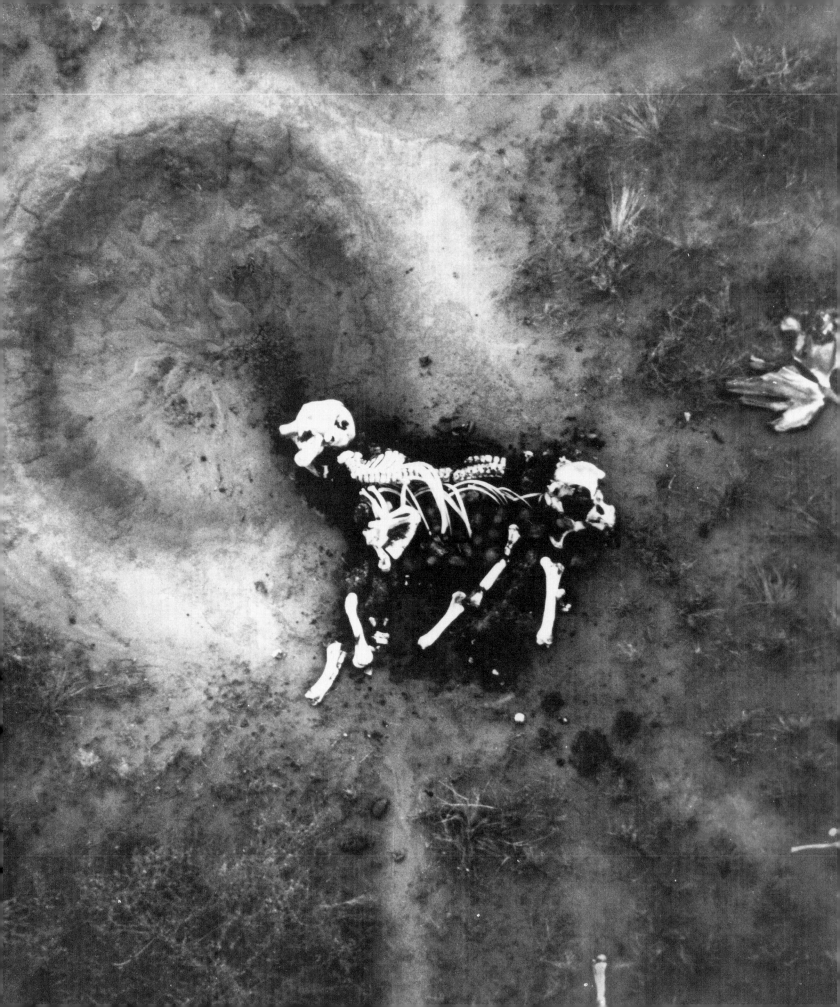

in clear terms with overwhelming figures to back it up, that *'The problem is overpopulation.'* And they were gotten rid of. It was obvious the truth was not wanted. Population is not one of the wildlife dramas that you can get all sentimental over when it comes to contribution time. Especially since it means destroying some of the population you love.

"It's like man possesses the reverse Midas touch. Everything we come in contact with, we destroy. The damage inside Tsavo—the crowding, manipulating, overgrazing, the explanations and excuses and then all the carcasses—was done by us. Everything from drought to corruption was blamed, all but the real cause of the destruction: human mismanagement."

Beard's thesis is defended by many, including Dick Laws, who went on to run the British Antarctic Survey after leaving Kenya. Laws defends his initial conclusions on Tsavo, as well as Beard's photographs. "The tragedy is that nothing appears to have been learnt from past mistakes. Beard has done a service to the cause of conservation by making a pictorial record which will continue to remind us that mistakes have occurred. This is his crime."

When Beard, Woodley, and I leave Tsavo I ask the retiring warden to predict the future of the park. He tries to be optimistic, though it's hard. He can remember when there were sixty-five thousand elephants here; now there are maybe five thousand. His biggest concern is another drought, which he is convinced will hit Kenya within the next decade, punishing this country as hard as Ethiopia, Somalia, and Sudan have been hit in recent years. But he is less concerned about the lives of animals than he is about the ever-expanding human population. With an annual growth rate of 4 percent, Kenya is the fastest-growing nation in the world. In 1983 its population stood at twenty million and was expected to double within fifteen years.

Leaving the park we drive across the Athi River, its waters rushing over the floorboards of the van. When we reach the opposite side, evidence of Woodley's concern is quickly apparent. We are met by a sprawl of huts, fences, and people. Woodley guesses that there are already thirty thousand cattle grazing illegally inside the park, and people will soon follow. It is not just the poor snatching up the land, either. Set aside for the local populace, much of this land has nonetheless been grabbed illegally by greedy cabinet ministers (including the former attorney general), senior civil servants, and party officials from Nairobi. Quietly observing the scene around him, Woodley says he believes 1963's independence was the beginning of the end for Kenya. "They've been *trying* for twenty-seven years now. At this rate, in twenty more the country will be in ruin."

"It's just all getting better," Beard mumbles, as we kick up dust, headed back to Nairobi.

The circle around this elephant carcass was created as the starving elephant writhed in agony for eight days before dying.

127

TEN

I think he's a terrific photographer and very charming.
He has enormous enthusiasm for everything he touches, he loves
people—and he's very good looking.

— DIANA VREELAND

He shows us Africa through young, vigorous, sophisticated New
York eyes and so we're paying attention.

— MARION JAVITS

Warhol at Hog Ranch

Peter is just wonderful; he always does the first things first.

— ANDY WARHOL

If Beard got comfortable in the bush in the sixties, the seventies were the years he grew comfortable in the limelight. His reputation as a world-class photographer was secured by a pair of New York city shows and the reissue of an updated *End of the Game.* His wunderkind reputation was upgraded to that of shaman, and he was surrounded in New York and Nairobi by beautiful people, especially beautiful women. His life began to get as much coverage as his photos, or more. In many ways the decade was a blur. "Beard first married Newport to East Africa, then he married Warhol to it," says filmmaker George Butler. "He considered informing people about Africa his job."

Beard's myth grew: It seemed everyone knew about his writing letters in his own blood, about his sticking the poacher in his own snare, about his years wandering in the bush. "He is a living relic, a reprise of those young Englishmen who in the 19th century went off to Africa to escape the coy hypocrisies of Victorian London and who, on returning—tanned, scarred, and storied—were surrounded by those who hoped to recharge themselves on their vigor," went one particularly sycophantic profile. Beard did little to dispel this evolving, romantic image of a young Tarzan with a brain flitting between New York and Nairobi and the world's jet-set capitals. He seemed always to be in the midst of a dozen different projects—books, films, collaborations—and inevitably surrounded by a gaggle of models and hangers-on.

Veruschka
von Lehndorff
in her *Blow-Up*
snakeskin leotard,
in Darajani,
1964

His passions in those years were many, and he was often to be found celebrating something, anything. One of the most infamous parties was a 1976 bash he hosted with Fleetwood Mac (the collage the band used on the cover of their "Tusk" album was his) at Studio 54, his seeming home-away-from-Hog Ranch, to raise money to buy elephants slated to be culled at South Africa's Kruger National Park. During the decade he collaborated with some of the era's best artists, working in a variety of mediums. He and Terry Southern wrote a screenplay based on *The End of the Game,* which was to be scored by the Rolling Stones. He worked with Andy Warhol on the "Batman" series. ("I got Andy into diaries," says Beard.) He was touted at a champagne breakfast at the Carlyle to launch *Longing for Darkness,* surrounded by Manhattan's most-chic. He dated Jackie Onassis's sister Lee Radziwill, palled around with Jackie's daughter, Caroline, and spent months on Ari Onassis's yacht. ("I hang about as the court jester," he wrote a friend, "and divert his maj with such pranks as—yesterday—winning a $2,000 bet by staying underwater for over 4 minutes . . . they love it and so do I.")

He made the cover of Warhol's *Interview* and had shows in Tokyo, Paris, and Arles. Carl Sagan selected one of his photographs to send up in the Voyager time capsule. In 1978 his fortieth birthday was celebrated at yet another legendary Studio 54 bash, this one highlighted by the lowering of a cake shaped like an elephant from the ceiling. Three hundred of his closest friends turned out to wish him well. He partied with the same fervor with which he had once attacked the Kenyan bush—endlessly, obsessively, and happily.

From a distance Beard seemed to be leading an inspired, charmed life. But anyone able to get close during these days saw a darker side. Even the fashion magazines caught a glimpse, one describing him as looking like "a rich kid on semester break from Yale . . . but up close a man of dark humor and fatalism." Nonetheless, it was an exhilarating, if slightly confusing, time for Beard. The hoopla heightened the allure of the high-society life he'd fled in the early 1960s, and on most days now he wrapped his arms around the scene, defending his society friends and his privilege.

On other occasions he wrestled publicly with his growing image as playboy/preservationist while being privately tormented by his instincts for a simpler life. He told *Interview* in 1977, "I'm just an unbelievably ordinary person. That is the horror of the whole thing. And anybody who tells you any different it's always in a direct ratio to the degree that they don't know me." He scoffed at the idea that he was rich: "I haven't got a dime. I have been in debt for twenty years. I have tiny little bits coming in, and several little tiny trusts, but it's like being on welfare." While having access to "tiny trusts" is hardly comparable to living on food stamps, Beard

Beard with Carrie Gammon, a neighbor and safari companion

130

never developed any real concept of money, neither how to make it nor how to spend it wisely. He was (and is) constantly in debt, and his pocketbook suffered from his spending time with real millionaires and trying to match their spending pace and lifestyle.

To escape the city, in 1972 he bought the last house on Long Island, at the tip of Montauk, for $130,000. The property comprised six acres, a small bungalow, and a trio of cottages. His first renovation was to purchase and truck in a 100-year-old windmill from six miles away. Perched on the cliffside overlooking the Atlantic Ocean, the mill became a refuge for New York City's beautiful people. The first summer he rented it to Halston in exchange for the designer's decorating help.

Beard of course added his own distinctive touches to his new home: a snake pit sat just off the wraparound deck and a cracked diving board jutted out over the cliff's edge. Skulls, bones, and snakeskins were scattered about the property, and he filled the walls inside with a valuable library of Africana and wildlife books, and paintings and watercolors by his friends, among them Richard Lindner, Francis Bacon, Warhol, and Andrew Wyeth. In these surroundings he was host to a nonstop party that starred Edward Albee, Richard Avedon (whom Beard eventually persuaded to buy the lot next door), Roy Lichtenstein, Dick Cavett, the Rolling Stones, the Bouvier sisters, Elia Kazan, Bianca Jagger, Beverly Johnson, Lauren Hutton, Veruschka, Truman Capote, Elizabeth Taylor, Maud Adams, Candice Bergen, and many others.

131

Lauren Hutton
at Hog Ranch,
1975

One thing Beard had long been renowned for was surrounding himself with gorgeous women, most of whom he was romantically linked with. This kind of notice, from *Cosmopolitan*'s "Tell All" page, fueled his reputation: "37-year-old Peter Beard, photographer-adventurer-socialite, can be found in New York or at his ranch in Kenya, photographing impala and leopards, often from his bedroom window! About women Peter says: 'I'm pathetically dependent on aesthetics. I'd like my best friend to be very visually pleasing.' Write him ℅ General Delivery, Montauk, NY."

His old bushmates in Africa were amazed by the beauties who traipsed to and through the bush with Beard. They surfaced in the early sixties, particularly Veruschka, one of the first models he photographed in Africa against the backdrop of wildlife. Throughout the sixties and seventies he photographed dozens of "beauties" for *Vogue, Harper's Bazaar,* and virtually every international fashion magazine in similarly unhampered settings. In most circles he was better known for those photos than for his books or wildlife pictures. He righteously defends his time spent squiring and photographing the world's most beautiful women against any critic: "I've always done fashion stuff if asked to . . . I like the girls, I like the extreme beauty. It always amazes me that I've been criticized for photographing both wildlife and beautiful women, because there is a thread between them: beautiful women will be the last thing left in nature that's worthy of worship."

One of his more outrageous feats during those years involved a beauty who is now one of the world's best known. "We planned the whole thing," he tells me late one night over *dawa*s (vodkas loaded with teaspoonfuls of sugar—the name means "medicine" in Swahili) at the Carnivore, a cavernous restaurant/disco outside Nairobi. The "we" he's talking about was he and a beautiful Somali girl named Imanyara Abdulmajid, more simply known as Iman.

132

Iman and a caravan of nomads, Lake Rudolf, 1986

The first photograph Beard took of Iman, in the bathroom of the studio

"I was driving in Nairobi one day [1975] and saw this amazing spectacle walking down the street. She was an acquaintance of Kamante's, Karen Blixen's manservant who had lived at Hog Ranch since 1962. I jumped from the Land Cruiser and approached her. She was remarkably beautiful and I said, 'Listen, I hope you're not going to waste all the incredible visuals.'"

She agreed to come to Hog Ranch to be photographed. She also explained that she would have to hide the photographing from her husband, a manager at the downtown Hilton. For several days she came to Hog Ranch and left by three-thirty, to be home before her husband.

Within weeks, in July 1975, Beard was introducing Iman to the world at a press conference in a borrowed Fifth Avenue apartment. "She is the most beautiful girl I have ever seen," he told the gathered press, adding that he had already arranged a contract for her with the Wilhemina modeling agency. The story he told was that he had discovered the six-foot-one-inch beauty in the northeastern desert of Kenya working as a goatherd, that she was unable to speak English and presumably possessed few social graces other than her God-given radiance.

Beard has long been an expert at promotion, of himself and others. Knowing that getting attention for the unknown model in a competitive market required a great sales pitch, the pair had agreed in advance to pad her biography. Iman was actually working for a Nairobi tour company when he first spotted her, a diplomat's daughter about to enroll at the University of Nairobi (and a mere five-foot-nine). At the time she quietly denied the exaggerations to anyone who listened, but she was savvy enough to realize her own potential. Years before she had escaped a rigid, chauvinistic life in Somalia by marrying a Kenyan; now she was anxious to escape her Kenyan life, too.

Beard's promotional instincts proved effective. The New York press raved about Iman, touting her as high fashion's first black African model. Wilhemina calculated how much she was worth and promoted her. "We had to simplify her origins because we needed to make an impact quick," says Beard, stirring his drink with the temple of his glasses. "When people found that she really wasn't from the bush, we got a second wave of press, and the second wave is what put her on the map. Besides, it was true that I'd run into her in the jungle . . . the jungle of Nairobi."

Today the pair has an unusual relationship. (On a recent Halloween he painted his face with shoe black and wore a badge on his sleeve that read "Discovered by Iman.") They are still friends, and Beard insists they were never more. "Initially I did everything for her. She had no papers when we met, no money, no agency, no place to stay." He also maintains

During a photo session at Hog Ranch a feisty giraffe bumped heads with Iman, knocking her to the ground and raising a large lump on her forehead.

there was never any financial gain for him in the relationship. In any case they share an intimacy those who have met her since cannot. He's traveled with her around Africa, back to the village where she was born. He knows where she came from and has seen her react to her own roots, a knowledge Beard claims is invaluable about any person, even himself.

. . . .

Much of the press and attention Beard received in the seventies was prompted by a pair of New York City shows. The first opened in December 1975 at the Blum Helman Gallery on Fifty-seventh Street. One entire wall was covered with contact sheets of diaries going back twenty-five years; another was covered with the haunting dead elephant photos. It was the public's first exposure to the eclectic, personal record of Beard's life and the destruction he'd witnessed. High society turned out by the limousine-load for the opening, and critics walked away open-mouthed. All were stunned but mostly overwhelmed by the eccentricity, the art, and the horror.

Two years later, in November 1977, came Beard's crowning moment, the opening of a one-man show at the International Center for Photography. It was the center's first one-person show, and Cornell Capa gave Beard the entire building to work with. Plotted with the help of noted designer Marvin Israel, the show shocked, disturbed, amused, and entertained, as well as cemented Beard's reputation as a photographer and artist. "The opening was the best night of his life," says a friend.

A seventy-five-foot-long photograph of a herd of elephants storming through a desolate African plain was wrapped around the building. On it was the title of the show: "The End of the Game: Last Word from Paradise." One of the largest ever printed, the photograph cost thousands out of Beard's own pocket and was blown to smithereens by high winds within hours of its installation. Beard loved that, metaphorically.

The walls on the first floor of the building were filled with pictures of diaries and live elephants. Upstairs the subject matter was solely dead elephants: The rooms were entered through a razor-stripped photograph of a live herd running away. There was even a twenty-foot-long elephant "swimming pool," with literally thousands of dead elephant photos collaged onto the floor under a huge piece of Plexiglas. At Beard's direction a squad of ten had spent a week pasting little pictures of dead elephants into a background.

The photographs, hung on dark brown walls, were illuminated by soft sepia lighting. Scattered throughout the building were display cabinets holding memorabilia such as books and artifacts, stuffed wild animals, pages ripped from diaries, display tables, and posters. Two short films Beard had made ran nonstop. Accompanying this tour of Beard's Africa were tape-

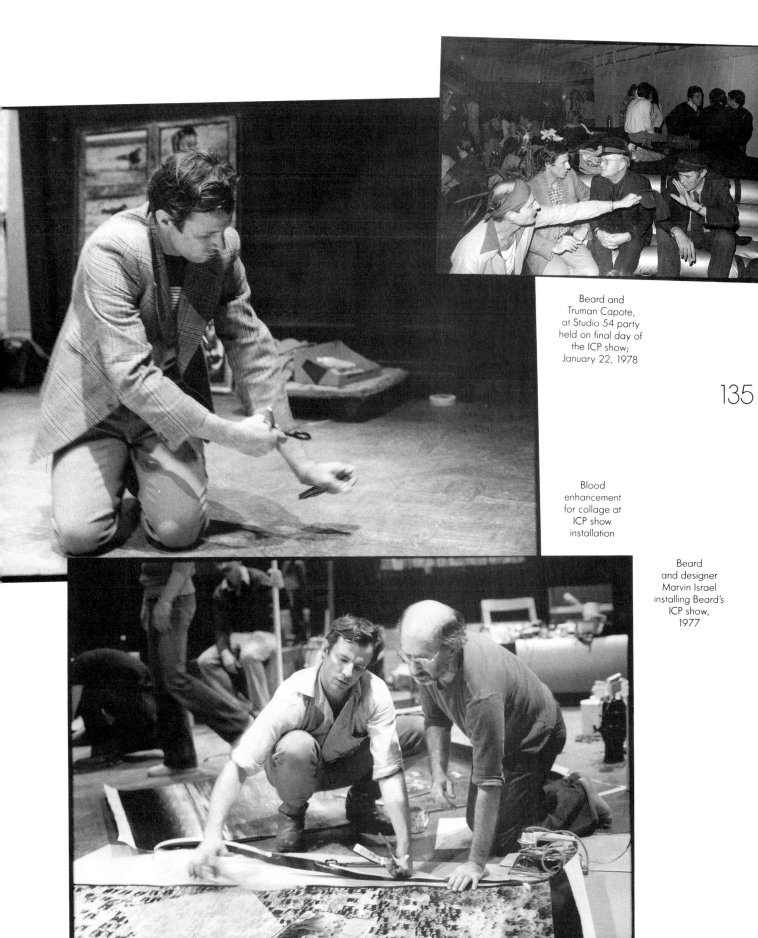

Beard and
Truman Capote,
at Studio 54 party
held on final day of
the ICP show;
January 22, 1978

135

Blood
enhancement
for collage at
ICP show
installation

Beard
and designer
Marvin Israel
installing Beard's
ICP show,
1977

the last word from paradise

The End of the Game
Peter H. Beard

recorded jungle sounds. The whole package offered a glimpse inside the artist's head.

"I had often considered the idea of having everything that's inside your head laid out on a wall, all at once," says Beard, talking about the show's conception. "I wondered how much room it would take. I mean, we have the most immense, organic computers ever created. That show revealed quite a lot of what was in mine."

In conjunction with the ICP show, Doubleday published a revised *End of the Game,* which brought Beard even more recognition. He was glad for the opportunity to revise the book, which was done initially as an "amateur swan . . . a corny homework assignment," he says. "I was relieved to be able to fix up a half-assed project that was unmistakably thrown together between classes. This new one encompassed twenty-three years of observations, collections, researches, photos, documentations. It was completely rewritten, completely redone." (While Doubleday printed and distributed the book, its revision—including hiring writer Steven Aronson and designer Ruth Ansel to help—cost Beard six figures out of his own pocket.)

The totally redesigned *End of the Game* included many new pictures, among them some from the collections of Archibald Roosevelt and Thomas Dinesen. It also included excerpts from the diaries of J. H. Patterson (builder of the Mombasa-to-Uganda railroad in the late 1890s), obtained for Beard by Caroline Kennedy. The text was stronger, more mature, and yet the youthful forecasting in the original turned out to be exceedingly accurate. This edition reflected a more wizened, experienced, darkly realistic Beard. Gone was the bravado and excitement of "the hunt." The foot safari he'd undertaken with Bill Du Pont was scrubbed almost entirely, and Du Pont's name nowhere to be seen. Wrote Beard in a new introduction: "This is the shadow of the end—the end of nature's processes, patterns, cycles, balances; all equilibrium and harmony destroyed. As boundaries are declared with walls and ditches, cement slowly suffocates the land; the great herds of the past become concentrated in new and strange habitats. Densities rise, the habitats are diminished, and the land itself begins to die. Imbalance is compounded. In the light of what has happened almost everywhere, in the face of thinner and thinner illusions, it can no longer be categorized as a wildlife book. It is a book about human behavior—in a world that once had coherent meaning."

He enlarged the section on Karen Blixen and included her kind words to him after reviewing his pictures in 1961: "Very few matters could move me as deeply as your epitaph, or monument over the Old Africa which was so dear to my heart—a continent of wisdom, dignity, and deep poetry, equally expressed in nature, beast, and man." And he added a letter he'd

Mockup of poster for the ICP show

received from Philip Percival before his death. "Why don't you take a good look at Tsavo," wrote Percival in 1963, "it's anybody's guess how the overall picture is going to develop—things are going pretty fast down there." The book's prologue was written by Joseph Murumbi, a former foreign minister and first vice president of Kenya: "For 20 years, Peter Beard has devoted himself to making this invaluable record. . . . But this is not a book of criticism as it is a book of art and enthusiasm to remind us that it is nature we are dismissing, literally overnight." An epilogue was written by Dick Laws, and Norman Borlaug, 1970 Nobel Prize winner and inventor of the Green Revolution, wrote an admiring blurb ("the only wildlife book I know that tells the truth"), as did Mary Hemingway ("belongs among the classics on East Africa, if not in a class by itself") and Murray Watson ("not only a disturbing record of progress in Africa, but also a metaphoric preview of human destiny"). The last chapter, originally a slightly optimistic view of Kenya's future called "The Great Hunter's Ball" was cut completely. It was replaced in the new version by a chapter titled "Nor Dread Nor Hope Attend," comprising solely pictures of dead elephants.

Reviews of the ICP show and of the new book were many and favorable. Robert Hughes, *Time*'s noted art critic, called Beard's body of work "'concerned' photography, with a twist. . . . Beard has in effect done for the elephant what the painter Francis Bacon—by no coincidence, the two men are close friends—did to the human body, but with the photographer's edge of documentary truth."

The message in both the new book and the shows was hardly optimistic. Rather, Beard had become resigned to what he saw as the inevitable end of nature. He hoped his pictures might shock his largely complacent and urbanized audience and provoke some reaction other than admiration for their maker. But many of Beard's new fans who flocked to the ICP didn't understand the ecological controversies behind the powerful images they were viewing. What they saw were dead elephants; most had no interest in how or why the animals died. Indeed, many loved the pictures in part because they loved the image of the photographer.

At the same time, among the serious wildlife crowd that moved between the States and Kenya there was criticism that somebody who spent half his time floating in the balmy heights of society and jetting around the globe could not possibly—or at least should not—be taken seriously. In truth, some of Beard's critics were privately jealous of his life and lifestyle (not to mention all those beautiful women). One result of such criticism was that the chasm between Beard's images and his reputation widened.

· · · · · · · · · · ·

The mid-1970s also saw the publication of Beard's third, and most eclectic, book: *Longing for Darkness,* a compilation of stories told by Karen Blixen's manservant, Kamante. Bringing Kamante to live at Hog Ranch was yet another of Beard's efforts to connect with the good old days.

Beard had found Kamante Gatura in 1962, with the help of Blixen herself and several of her former staffers still living around Nairobi. He and the staffers drove to the village of Rengute, where Kamante had been born, and found him sitting on a stone wall as if he'd been expecting them. "I presented him with a letter from Baroness Blixen and got a rumpled chicken in return," says Beard. "He then guided me to Mbogani, or Karen House." Beard encouraged Kamante and his family to come live with him.

Kamante's life had been both blessed and cursed. Employed by Blixen when he was nine, he was wracked by painful sores on his legs that she encouraged him to have cured. He eventually became her cook and one of the most memorable characters in *Out of Africa.* When Blixen left Kenya she provided for a farm for Kamante, twelve acres plus chickens in Rengute, and since her departure he had spent his days grazing and selling cattle, and drinking. In the 1950s he spent a year in prison for taking the Mau Mau oath. When Beard found him he was over sixty and married to the same woman, Wambui, he'd wed on Karen's farm in the 1920s.

Kamante's remembrances of those days, along with watercolors he painted, were the basis of *Longing for Darkness.* Together with Abdullahi (featured in Blixen's *Shadows of Grass*), Saufe Aden (mentioned in *Out of Africa*), and three of his sons, Kamante spoke his stories (he could neither read nor write) into a tape recorder between 1962 and 1968. Told in Swahili, they were then transcribed, edited, and illustrated by close relatives under Beard's direction.

Kamante remembered Kenya the way Beard preferred it to be remembered: "Before the farm was ploughed out many animals were coming

139

Kamante and Beard with Karen Blixen's former staffers, at Rengute Village

140

Kamante
and his wife,
Wambui

Kamante
and his family
at Hog Ranch,
1960s

from many places—buffaloes, leopards, hippopotamus, monkeys. But all animals got lost from the farm because people had built houses everywhere with cattle and they were holding night dances of old men, women and young men, and the noise was great." "Karen was everything for me," he said, "and when Karen died it was like my father and mother had died. I feel I am the son of Karen." Not coincidentally, *Longing for Darkness* concludes with Kamante's telling of the death of Denys Finch Hatton.

"Till Kamante's death he could tell a story with great glances and epic pauses," wrote Judith Thurman, "and he is still a figure 'half of fun and half of diabolism.' Sometimes I had the feeling he was really impersonating himself for me—playing the outcast, the destiné, the jester, the muse and servant of a great artist." Needless to say, Kamante and Beard got along famously.

Their book of real-life fables was not easy to sell to New York publishers. It wasn't until Jackie Onassis offered to help and ended up writing an afterword that the book was finally taken by Harcourt Brace Jovanovich. Beard received a $35,000 advance, which he says barely covered his years of expenses on transcription, artwork, transportation, and so forth.

Beard's myth took on new dimensions shaped by disaster as well as success. Just prior to the ICP show—July 28, 1977—his Montauk windmill burned to the ground in a spectacular fire that could be seen from across Long Island Sound in Connecticut. Beard was in New York finalizing the new *End of the Game* when an improperly installed oil burner exploded, igniting the basement's oil storage tanks.

The fire destroyed everything inside the mill: thousands of photographs, an expensive new darkroom, his library of rare books, his art collection, and twenty years worth of diaries. The loss was estimated at between $250,000 and $1 million. Only a melted sculpture of a lion was left standing, and only the inside pages of some of the diaries, their edges burned, survived. Fortunately, Beard had recently photographed some of the diary pages for the ICP show; in the show he displayed several of the burned remnants.

Ironically, Beard did not visit the ruin for a month, making himself too busy in New York. What was taken by many to be an indication of callousness was in fact a measure of his heartbreak. Although his façade is one of nonchalance toward the material, the fire was a major loss and, in retrospect, was a forewarning of troubled years ahead. Today the mill still sits tumbled in its cement foundation; Beard agonizes that he's never had the money to rebuild it.

142

. . . .

Another tragedy of the late seventies began as a high point. It involved yet another woman, perhaps America's most famous beauty at the time.

In the bathroom of the Hog Ranch studio is a five-shelf bookcase crammed with stacks of magazines—*Time, Interview, Vogue, Private Eye, Swara, True Confessions*—piled in seemingly random order. But taped to one shelf, in Beard's handwriting, is a terse request: "Please put it back where it came from." Scribbled beneath his plea for order, in a feminine script that can only be described as cute, are two words: "Yes Sir." The response is signed "CTB," Cheryl Tiegs Beard.

Of all the well-known women Beard has been associated with over the years it is perhaps his dalliance with, and subsequent marriage to, supermodel Tiegs for which he is best known by the masses (better known, to his immense chagrin, than for his books or photographs). He can't tell me much about his second wife, however, though I sense he is itching to. For weeks after they divorced (after four years), he carried around a photocopy that he passed out whenever anyone asked about Cheryl. It read simply: "Under the terms of his divorce agreement, Peter Beard is forbidden to talk about Cheryl Tiegs." The half-million-dollar, eighty-seven-page divorce decree specifically states that he can say nothing about their relationship or marriage. He isn't even supposed to utter her name until 1993. The little that I was able to learn about their affair comes from published accounts.

They met in New York in 1978 and got to know each other better during shoots for ABC's "American Sportsman" in Kenya. Tiegs was then married to adman Stan Dragoti and was both a household face in the United States and a multimillionairess. In Africa, though, she was on unfamiliar ground. She respected Beard's knowledge of his adopted home, as well as his nonstop desire to have fun, and they became an item. Once she was officially divorced, they married, in May of 1981, in Montauk. The years that followed were split between Hog Ranch, Montauk, and Cheryl's three-bedroom Park Avenue duplex. At the time she was making upwards of $350,000 a year modeling, and her "CT" clothing label was racking up $100 million in annual sales at Sears.

The relationship had some sizable ups and downs, literally from the day they were married. When they were in the States, Tiegs saw Beard as no longer king of the castle, as he was at Hog Ranch and in Kenya. In the States Tiegs was the breadwinner and the better known of the pair. Steven Aronson, in the first chapter of his 1988 *Hype,* wrote: "There were times when they reminded friends of those novelty barometers out of which pop a gloomy boy when the weather is foul and a beaming girl when the outlook is fair. Once, in a driving rainstorm, Beard threw Tiegs's entire

143

Cover of *Interview,*
February 1978

wardrobe out the window onto the lawn. A few days later, Tiegs locked Beard out of her suite at the Carlyle in the early hours of the morning. He repaired to a friend's couch.

"Within the year Tiegs was introducing Beard, only half in jest, as 'the second best husband I've ever had.'" When they finally divorced, Tiegs stripped everything—everything—out of the Montauk house, including Beard's collected art works and African paraphernalia.

Beard today is cynical about marriage (though apparently happy in his third, which has lasted six years). One day, sitting at Lake Rudolf as the sun set, feet dug into the sand, Tusker in hand, he reminisced about the first two. About Minnie he said: "I was so stupid. I should have waved good-bye as soon as she left Africa; instead, I wasted nearly a year chasing her. Like an idiot I tried to hang on and it didn't work out. My advice now is get that first one behind you. By comparison, when the second one was fading [Beard divorced Tiegs], I just said with a delighted smile, 'Okay, see you.'"

His thoughts on marriage ironically mirror those of Denys Finch Hatton, who once said: "Remember, when you are sure in your heart that you have done everything you can to make your marriage a success, *in all sincerity,* and it still does not work, then you must leave as soon as possible, for it is merely weakness to go on trying."

. . . .

For all the good reviews and the good times that came his way during the decade, in some people's eyes Beard—just like his beloved Kenya— suffered during the late seventies. He spent more time in New York than in Nairobi, was as often to be seen in the south of France as in the bush. The dichotomy made it hard for many conservationists to take him seriously; his visionary status was threatened by his steady appearance in the gossip columns.

Perhaps most important, those years saw him essentially set aside his wildlife camera. For reasons he will only hint at—primarily that photographers aren't taken seriously as artists—he essentially gave up writing and photography and upped the preaching. He began to present himself as a man of opinion, not just a photographer or bookmaker.

It was curious timing, coming at the very moment he was starting to get notoriety because of his photos. Interesting, too, he was being applauded for his visionary take on Africa at a time when he was spending fewer and fewer days there. The contradiction was caught by some. According to writer Larry Shames: "Basically he was partying his way toward Armageddon, and doing it in the best of company . . . he lived with Cheryl Tiegs while railing against the crass commercialism of pop culture,

bivouacked at the Hotel Carlyle while complaining that he lacked the cash
to get his pictures printed, and spewed venom at the 'pompous, pretentious,
tight-assed art establishment' while munching cold lobster at Les Pleiades,
nerve center of New York's uptown gallery scene."

Beard perhaps better than anyone recognized the contradictory aspects
of his life. If questioners really listened, they heard his desire to be taken
seriously. "I would like to be able to say that I am one of those great
missionaries and martyrs that everybody loves," he told one reporter in
1978. "I think people are interested in my books because they think I am
a do-gooder. But my concerns are quite the opposite, selfish and rather
unattractive. I'm just trying to scrape through." He truly regarded himself
and his work as exceedingly "ordinary." In many respects he would have
liked to unshoulder the acclaim and retreat into the African bush, reverting
somehow to the good old days. But those days were past and the future
was spinning faster and faster, beyond his control. For Beard, the eighties
would be both exhilarating and frightening.

ELEVEN

What singles Beard out so unmistakeably from the mechanized army
that roars and clicks across Africa is the same thing that
singled out Ahab from the average sea captain—a kind of
madness. The eye that peers through his lens is not your Garden
of Eden variety rational optic; it is estranged from the world of
impeccable boundaries, and its hallucinatory perceptions transfigure
his pictures. They become messages sent from the Apocalypse.

— OWEN EDWARDS, *Village Voice*

Any Fool Can Take a Picture

It is early on a spring morning, and we've been in the Hog Ranch studio
for hours, looking at pictures and paging through books. Beard becomes
fascinated with a dozen books seemingly at once and piles them open in
front of me, pointing out paragraphs and pages I *must* read, immediately.
"Oh this is great, you'll love this," he says.

While it is often difficult to pierce Beard's protective armor, inherited
from generations of ultra-guarded WASPs, much of his personality and
experience is evidenced by his collected paraphernalia. The studio—with
its white walls, parquet floor, double bed, flush toilet, floor-to-ceiling
mirror, and a fig tree growing through its roof—is laden with stuff he's
collected over the past three decades. Musty and dusty from underuse, every
corner lends insight to Beard's years, successes, travails, and fears. Piles of
books and magazines and correspondence cover the tables, chests, floor,
and shelves. Photographs of native women are tacked to the wall next to
blowups of old girlfriends. Back copies of *Vogue* mingle with UNEP reports;
anthologies of Picasso and Bacon sit spine-to-spine with African history
books (like Frederick Selous's *African Nature Notes and Reminiscences*).

Stones, bones, and skulls of all sizes litter every flat surface, as do
photos of living buffaloes, elephants, crocodiles, and a pair of copulating
giraffes. A Beard portrait of Jomo Kenyatta hangs next to a skinned carcass,
which hangs next to a photo of Jackie Onassis. Framed covers of *Newsweek*
boast the visages of Hog Ranch visitors, including Jean Shrimpton and
Cheryl Tiegs. From an overhead beam hangs a pink tutu, Masai necklaces,
beaded chest plates, cowbells, and more shells and bones. From a nail hangs
Denys Finch Hatton's empty camera case.

Photograph of
Bacon on the
Thames by Beard
on one of his
frequent visits,
1972

147

A record album recorded by Beard's cousin Jerome Hill is nailed to one wall, surrounded by a snapshot of Richard Leakey, watercolors by Kamante, and a wanted poster for the assassin of J. M. Kariuki. Polaroids, prints, and contact sheets spill out of drawers and wicker baskets or are crudely stacked on the floor. Thirty years worth of yellow legal pads sit in heaps, every page filled to the edge with Beard's scribbling and drawings, letters, notes, and manic doodling.

The studio
at Hog Ranch

Bookshelves wrap the room, sagging with a valuable collection of Africana. Removed from the shelf and cracked open, each book rains photographs, snapshots, leaves, dried insects, matchbooks, letters, postcards, newspaper clippings, and magazine pictures, all placed there by Beard at the time he read or carried that particular tome around with him. The first third of each book is underlined and marked with comments, phone numbers, and names of friends (apparently Beard's random attention span does not allow him to complete most books). Poems, favorite quotes, and clippings are glued or taped inside front and back covers and are usually unrelated to the book's subject. Most of the books are inscribed inside the cover: "P. Beard, Nairobi" (or "Montauk"); many are signed by his own hand- or footprints in India ink, mud, or blood.

For the variety of stuff in the room, for the authenticity it lends to a broad and much-lived life, what dominates still are his photographs, nailed and thumbtacked to the walls and scattered about the floor. Whatever else Beard tries to tell you, no matter what avenues he persists on trying to steer you down in his eternal efforts to deny the label, he is first and foremost an accomplished photographer. It is his truest talent and skill, though he consistently downplays it. His lectures about conservation ethics, his theories on wildlife and population dynamics—those are based on information mostly learned from the studies or writings of others. The photographs, especially the collages he makes from what he calls "subject matter," are all his. Even so, he continually attempts to distance himself from a reputation as simply a photographer.

His disclaimers notwithstanding, he has produced pictures more memorable and with a more haunting beauty than have most serious photographers. Three of his pictures were covers of *Life,* yet he says "photographs mean nothing to me." Like certain other offhandedly gifted photographers, he is better than he knows. As one critic put it, Beard "lacks theory, but he sees." If he is guilty of anything, it is of not taking photography seriously enough; his long-held belief is that "any fool can take a picture."

Leaning back in a wooden chair pulled up to a plywood table, he laughs at the "gadget-phobia" that dominates the lives of most photographers. "I think photography should be something you use, not that uses you. If it's your career, if you're a professional photographer, I think you're in real serious trouble. They are victims of commercial markets and the fact their lives aren't being lived anymore, they're just that little sickly white piece of flesh behind the lens."

In truth Beard wishes he had chosen the path of a more serious artist, that rather than photography he'd devoted himself to painting, for example,

149

which he studied at Yale. His opinion? "Photography simply doesn't have the dynamic or scope or depth. Photography is technological, not the exposure of the whole nervous system like art is."

"While I love the magic of photography . . . I don't think photos have the same impact as a work that's been individually attended to by an artist who draws, paints, scrapes, carves, et cetera. I love the ease, speed, and distance of photography, but there's far more information in a real work of art, about the painter and subject. A photo is like a collected stone; it's what you do with it that matters.

"I wouldn't walk across the street to worship a Weston. I've seen those green peppers of his so many times they're coming out of my ears. How about Karsh? That fuzzy, oily Hemingway? Nuns on the beach, cats, reeds, old people's wrinkles—all that self-seriousness, faithful predictability, Magnum photography, *yyuuuck*—except Robert Capa. They're all so dedicated . . . so politically correct!

"Photography should be something you just love to do, the subject matter something you can make something of. If you use pictures artistically, then maybe you've done something artistic.

"Myself, I don't worship a single frame. I've never really believed in the constipated overuse of single photographic images. Of course there are some exceptions, like just about anything taken by Julia Margaret Cameron.

"Occasionally others—like Lartigue, occasionally Cartier-Bresson, Mathew Brady, and Les Krims (who makes Diane Arbus, as wonderful as she was, look like she could have had more scope) make incredible single images, so artistic you'd have to say they fall into the category of art. Maybe so with Avedon's photograph of Eisenhower, or that kid with a tree that looks like a bomb. I also like the painters who took photographs, like Vuillard, Degas, Eakins, Sidney Nolan, David Hockney, Marcel Duchamp.

"But is photography art? No way. A photograph, framed and hanging in the archives, might be equal to a few brush strokes from Picasso. Those desert photos by the Westons and Paul Strand and everybody else *all together* could be equaled by a few dozen brush strokes from Matisse or Bacon—strokes which would come directly from their highly tuned brain onto the picture surface. One only has to look at Rauschenberg or Warhol or Bacon or Duchamp or even Lucas Samaras to realize how tragic are the faithful activities of the Sierra Clubbers out there in the wastelands of their minds photographing dunes and pebbles with plodding dedication.

"Great paintings seem to paint themselves; great photographs accumulate over a period of time. Discipline and lyrical spirit combine in the end to let quality flow out on its own. Great things aren't forced,

152

contrived, or manipulated. But there are no rules. If there is one, it's to consider the opposite of whatever you might think.

"My advice is if you want to find work in photography, find something important in life . . . something original, something personal, something that takes you out on a limb of exploration in a direction which grows in force from its own consistency and momentum and accumulative rhythms and themes . . . something from your nervous system rather than your intellect . . . something that isn't clever or clichéd or contrived or left over from school. Not more of those old women and babies crying behind rained-on window panes, cracks in the walls, the artist in his studio and the horrors of war. . . ."

Beard is convinced that without a personal obsession, photography is little more than snapshooting homework. His theory is that great subject matter begets good photographs, which then become part of the artist's collected vision.

"I'm not a message bearer, but I like the idea of documentation and then use, in a sort of collage over a period of time. One of the reasons I like photography is simply to grab on to things that are being lost forever in the fast-changing world. Photography is a good way to snatch it now in this speedy world and we're very lucky to have the invention."

Perhaps no critic has viewed Beard's photography more insightfully over the years than Owen Edwards: "How can photography deal with Peter Beard?" he wrote in 1975. "He is a self-proclaimed amateur who periodically careens like a fireworks pinwheel into the decorous scheme of things, strewing incandescent images and making earnest barn-side photographers and seekers-after-grants look plodding and ordinary. Even as his pictures force themselves into the most protected preserves of our minds, he insists that they are incidental, nothing more than the most convenient medium for his narrative purposes. Yet despite his blue-blooded offhandedness, Beard can no longer easily be ignored.

"In the end, it's the photographs that count. Beard is not our Pepys, but he may be our Gibbons. What started as a schoolboy jaunt in the general direction of adventure has become a photographic odyssey across a vast landscape of death. He is not talking about conserving a few species . . . what he is showing us in his pictures is far more than Kenya and elephants; he is showing us downtown Detroit, the South Bronx, the earth and ourselves. . . . By this measure, Peter Beard's massive gray monoliths, gutted and rotting on their self-made desert, are photographic art at its most transfiguring. Even more terrifying, they are the shapes of things to come."

153

Beard is not alone in his concern about overrating photography or using photographic images to shape opinion. Robert Frank worried in very similar terms. "I have been frequently accused of deliberately twisting subject matter to my point of view," Frank wrote in 1958. (Beard has often been accused of the same.) "Above all, I know that life for a photographer cannot be a matter of indifference." Though Beard and Frank have focused on very different subjects—the former the demise of Africa, the latter the condition of America—there is a bond between the two. Judging by his African pictures, no one can suggest Beard has led a "life of indifference."

• • • • • • • • • • •

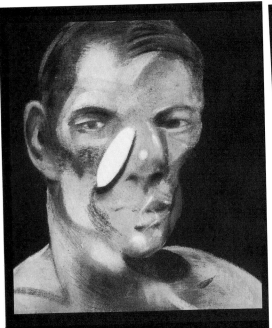 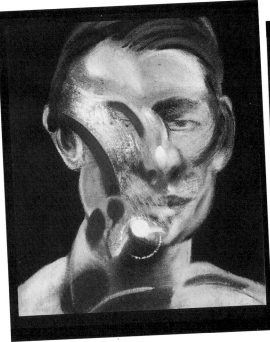 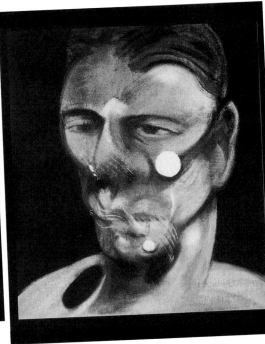

Francis Bacon, Three Studies for a Portrait of Peter Beard, 1971

Throughout Beard's discourses on photography, art, and life the name that pops up most frequently is that of Francis Bacon. The eighty-two-year-old English painter, whom many consider one of the greatest of the twentieth century, was both his mentor and friend. "He and Picasso are the ultimate painter's painters, twentieth-century Van Goghs," Beard proclaims. Bacon died in Madrid in April 1992.

The two were introduced in London in the mid-sixties, at the opening of a show of Bacon's at Marlborough, to which Beard went hoping to shake his idol's hand. "I saw him standing there, went up and said something like 'Hello, Peter Beard, happy to meet you, just came to see the show.' Luckily he clicked. He'd gotten a copy of *The End of the Game,* which really shocked me. That's the best thing that book ever did for me! I have no idea how he got it, or remembered it, but he told me he wanted to do sculptures based on some of the photographs, which blew my mind. I'd been a Bacon follower since I went to school in England in 1956. Though he never made much of an effort, I made sure to stay in touch with him over the years. He was always an oasis of inspiration and clarity."

Beard found irresistible and adopted many of the painter's philosophies and phraseologies. "We are all carcasses" is a favorite Bacon theme that Beard gladly borrows; so are his frequent references to "working directly off one's nervous system" and "subject matter." (Here's Bacon on "subject matter": "The obsession with something in life that you want to record gives a much greater tension and a much greater excitement than when you've simply said you'll just go on in a free-fancy way and record the shapes and the colours.")

Beard also thrives on the fact that Bacon painted from a variety of his pictures of wildlife (and on several dozen occasions even painted Beard. In 1989 a triptych of Beard by Bacon sold for $2.25 million). Not one to hasten from extremes, Beard holds Bacon's views of art and life as *the truth*. "Everything Bacon said was pure and clear, concentrated, deeply honest, because he had thought everything out. He dwelled on the artificiality of life, the unnaturalness of humans, our distance from nature.

"I think the world that looms up in Bacon's paintings, even though he didn't intend it to be, is the most haunting essence of man's future. We will soon be as severely cornered, freaked, frightened and stressed and strung-out and screaming as his fleshy, writhing, nervous systems of mutated, skinned-out carcasses seem to appear. His howling businessmen, gangsters, and popes will be calling out the future as realistically as these thousands of starving, rotting, cornered, grinning dead elephants."

155

Double exposure
of Francis Bacon
with the
Peter Beard
triptych

TWELVE

But past who can recall or done undo.

— JOHN MILTON,
Paradise Lost

The Disaster Years

What Beard witnessed in Kenya in the 1970s—the die-off of tens of thousands of elephants, the ravaging of paradise—changed the way he looked at everything from preservation to procreation, from the power of photography to his own complexities. He had come to Africa because he loved *everything* about it: the promise of adventure, the vast space, the romance of the colonials, the abundant wildlife, the diversity, the freedom. But the more he saw, the more he learned. Losses were far outstripping gains. As he repeatedly points out today, every place he focused his camera it seemed things were fading and dying.

His reaction in the 1980s was to increase his efforts to get deeper into the bush. Leica in hand, his attentions turned from wildlife to wild people. He concentrated on photographing human beauty in new, bizarre locations: Iman next to a variety of wild beasts (including copulating gerenuks and snarling lions) or Janice Dickinson lying atop crocodiles and cheetahs. Art directors loved the work, and assignments came from *Playboy, Paris Match, Elle, Photo,* and the German, French, and Italian editions of *Vogue.*

For himself he focused on photographing the people of Africa, particularly the Masai. His fondness for the Masai, out of the forty-plus tribes in Kenya, was related to the fact that Hog Ranch abuts Masai land and that they were Karen Blixen's favorite Africans.

Beard also spent the eighties polishing his skills with moving pictures. Peugeot, for one, hired him to direct television commercials set in Kenya's bush.

He had worked with film crews around Africa on many occasions before, but usually as technical consultant, not director. (He had played featured roles on ABC's "American Sportsman" a half dozen times.) Being asked to direct TV commercials was a great opportunity for him to dust off his accumulated bush experiences and apply them to a different medium. It also gave the crews he worked with a chance to witness his rare understanding of how to work with big animals in the bush. Cinematographer Bert Van Munster claims he's never seen anyone in the bush as comfortable working with animals as Beard.

Janice Dickinson
(helping Beard pay for
lawyers' expenses),
1985

In 1988, with a crew of twenty, he took a fire-engine red Peugeot station wagon into remote parts of Kenya and along the Tanzanian border and shot the car weaving through a running herd of over two hundred elephants. At Solio Ranch in the Highlands north of Nairobi, he encouraged an old friend—Rudi the rhinoceros, whom he had helped trap back in the early 1960s with Ken Randall—to gallop alongside the moving car. The rhino was bigger than the Peugeot, and to lure him close enough to the vehicle Beard hung out the window enticing him with a stalk of sugar cane. At one point his hand disappeared into the rhino's mouth, which gave him quite a scare, for he'd once seen Rudi chomp a ranger's finger off for the same miscalculation.

Two solid years—1986 and 1987—were dominated by the production and filming of an hour-long television special for ABC ("Peter Beard in Africa: Last Word from Paradise"). The resulting prime-time show provided him, his photographs, and his eco-philosophies access to a huge new audience, estimated at twenty-two million.

The $1-million production sent Beard and a crew crisscrossing Kenya for four solid months in 1987, filming the people and places that had framed his understanding of Africa. While somewhat uncomfortable in front of the camera (they ate up an hour of expensive film just trying to get him to say "Hi, I'm Peter Beard" without breaking into tears of laughter), his contributions as a guide and educator were invaluable. With Mbuno and Galo-Galo he tracked elephants on the Mara and visited the elephants' graveyard in Tsavo East; toward Mombasa, at the mouth of the

Tana River, he photographed a rare riverbuck; and with raptor expert Simon Thomsett he helped capture and release a rare crowned eagle. They filmed in Nairobi National Park, on the shores of Lake Rudolf, at Hog Ranch, in Amboseli, and at Cottar's Camp on the Athi River. The finished film offered Beard's impressions of Kenya in the late eighties and gave him a rare opportunity to spread his message about overpopulation and the hazards of sentimental fundraising. The show also served as a pilot for a hoped-for series of shows he would host in environmentally endangered spots around the globe.

The downside of the ABC production was the mid-February goring of Terry Mathews. A thirty-year friend of Beard's, the professional hunter and safari guide had been hired for two days to guide Beard and the TV crew as they tracked a mother and baby pair of rhinos through Nairobi National Park. As two cameras filmed Beard and Mathews approaching the rhinos, a vanload of boisterous tourists distracted the big beasts and the mother advanced in the direction of the humans. Beard reversed his position, but Mathews stood his ground, desperately picking up stones off the ground and hurling them at the two-ton beast, shouting at the top of his lungs, "Bugger off! Go on, bugger off!" Unfortunately, the park ranger carrying a rifle had gone off to try and quiet the tourists. When the rhino got close, Mathews turned to run, but tripped in his sandals and fell to the ground. Inexplicably, he stood up again, allowing the rhino a clean shot at his body. In one quick motion the rhino impaled Mathews through the left hip, tossing him high into the air like a rag doll.

Mathews was alive but badly injured. The rhino's horn had sliced between his kidney and spleen, plunging up under his ribs and stopping a quarter of an inch from his heart. His left leg was fractured and three vertebrae were broken. Doctors had to split his body open from neck to knee to investigate the damage. He spent months in the hospital, unsure whether he would ever walk again. Shortly after he was released, Mathews and his family sued ABC, Beard, and Beard's agent, Peter Riva, who was executive producer of the production, claiming they were all responsible for his injuries. For obvious reasons the suit was controversial and has grown acrimonious. It has also split the white community of Kenya in two. Most of the old white hunter crowd has sided with Mathews; those who have seen the actual footage side with Beard.

Tony Archer, longtime friend of both men and technical adviser on the ABC production, spoke about the accident one night around Beard's campfire. The aftermath has cost him Mathews's friendship. "The smart thing you did that day, Peter," he said, "was wear good running shoes."

Beard's reputation is not for running from trouble. One night in 1985, while camped on the Masai Mara, he witnessed a violent attack by *shiftas* (bandits). He was tenting near a safari camp when he heard screams; bandits had attacked a group of German and Dutch tourists. Wielding a *panga* in one hand and his camera in the other, Beard chased after the fleeing thieves, swinging the machete and using his camera as a club. The results were bloody: One visitor lost several fingers, another's thigh was opened wide. Beard drove the bloodied tourists four hours to the hospital. His pictures of the night—tents and clothing soaked in fresh blood—are vivid reminders that in today's Kenya man has little to fear from wild animals but much to fear from his own species.

160

Peugeot commercial, Kimana, 1988

· · · · · · · · · · ·

For all the adventures and high times, the Mathews controversy was emblematic of the eighties for Beard, who found himself embroiled in a maelstrom of controversies, including lawsuits, arrests, shouting matches, and newspaper headlines. While he continued to speak out about the mismanagement of Kenya's wildlife (he dubbed it "the ongoing wildlife Watergate") and its portent for the future, many of his days were spent defending himself against wildlife society critics and local witch-hunts.

Sadly, all these controversies tended to overshadow Beard's most fervent forecast, that expanding human populations were endangering the planet's future. His oft-repeated, nightmarish predictions—that because of mismanagement and overcrowding man would someday suffer the same tragic end as the elephants of Tsavo—were being borne out in countries neighboring Kenya, especially Ethiopia and Somalia, where millions were starving to death. He grew increasingly sarcastic as his predictions turned into truths, yet his continued harangues fell on deaf ears.

162

Mel Stuart and
Beard working on the
ABC-TV special,
Hog Ranch,
1987

Today, if you hang around Beard long enough, you invariably pick up a colloquial smattering of Swahili. But before you learn *tafathali* (please), *asante* (thank you), or *kwaheri* (good-bye), you must know *fitina* (gossip, rumors, trouble). In an odd way he seems to thrive off the negative energy of *fitina*s and controversy.

The *fitina*s reached a crescendo in 1985, which Beard called "the worst year of my life." Twice he was jailed in Nairobi, on eight different charges ranging from growing pot to trafficking in "abscene [sic] literature." For several weeks he was forced to live at the Intercontinental Hotel, after the CIA warned him that his life was in danger if he stayed at Hog Ranch. Jailed on two consecutive weekends, he was handcuffed to another prisoner who was then badly beaten. "You're next, *mzungu* [white man]," threatened the guards.

After some carefully scattered bribes and detective work by Beard and friends, it became apparent that somebody with connections wanted to grab Hog Ranch. In retrospect it is obvious that the move to "confiscate" the valuable piece of property—by means of police raids, seizure of personal property, and trumped-up charges headlined in the government-run *Kenya Times*—was instigated by persons close to the president. It wasn't personal, Beard says today, but purely business. His forty-five acres would make a prime location for a development of expensive homes and townhouses.

"Eventually, it all comes 'round to Hog Ranch," Beard says one gorgeous mid-afternoon. We are sitting outside the mess tent, the sun setting slowly over the Ngongs. His tone is jocular, even though he is remembering a particularly tragic time, one he readily admits was a frightening time, too. People are killed in Kenya for far less than forty-five acres of valuable land. What prompts our conversation is that it is the sixth anniversary (June 1) of the first of several police raids on Hog Ranch intended to scare him out of Kenya for good.

The memories are prompted, too, by a visit from a Somali model named Amina. She had been at Hog Ranch the Saturday in 1985 when that first raid took place. Beard was photographing a former Miss Africa, Khadija Adam, who, fortunately, spoke perfect Kikuyu and understood what the plainclothes police were saying when they arrived in force. They had come, without a warrant, to search the place for anything incriminating for which they could arrest the American. Beard and the models fled the property before any arrests could be made, leaving behind an elaborate note explaining that he would reply to any proper search warrant. Afterward it was reported to Beard by his staff that the leader of the police raid was married to one of Kamante's daughters. It soon became clear that the harassment was being assisted by insiders, including relatives of Kamante, particularly his son, Francis Kimani.

Kamante's family was worried that once Kamante died—the eighty-four-year-old man was paralyzed from a stroke—they would be eased off Hog Ranch. Intent on getting title to part or all of Hog Ranch, Francis Kimani had put the land grab into motion by going to a Nairobi real estate company and inquiring as to what the property was worth. Delighted that the valuable property might be for sale, the realtors went ahead and made a bid ($150,000) that Beard kindly turned down, saying that he didn't want to sell.

When Francis Kimani took it upon himself to try to "encourage" Beard to leave Kenya, the realtors—who had friends in high places in Kenya's government—did not discourage his mildly unsophisticated plan. At one point he delivered to Beard a handwritten extortion note requesting six million KSH, or about $300,000 ("Six million will do very nicely," it read), for back payment to Kamante and his share of profits from *Longing for Darkness.* Beard argued that he didn't owe Kamante anything and that their book had never earned any money.

The realtors pursued their own course of harassment, aided by the police and the government. They realized that if Beard was found guilty of any felony, the 1962 exemption granted by Jomo Kenyatta that allowed the American to own Hog Ranch would be rescinded and he would forfeit the land. Even a short jail sentence would mean deportation. It was hardly coincident that the first time Beard was arrested was two weeks after turning down a second offer (of $200,000) from the realtors.

Over the course of nine months he was arrested twice (both at 4 P.M. on Friday, so there was no chance to bail him out before the weekend) and harassed repeatedly. The first jail time was on a charge of trafficking in "abscene [sic] literature." During the initial raid on Hog Ranch police had seized a catalog from the Museum of Modern Art in Paris. On the cover was a Helmut Newton photograph of an opera singer in the mouth of a crocodile. (Beard hadn't seen the show; Newton had sent him the catalog.) Police claimed she was "improperly dressed" and charged him with possession of pornography.

The second arrest was for allegedly growing marijuana, a charge accompanied by banner headlines in the *Kenya Times* that read "40 Acre Bhang Garden Found in Langata." The marijuana was actually found in a ten- by twelve-inch plot near one of the staff's cabins, and the evidence shown Beard at the police station was four inches high, withered, and with no soil on its obviously dead roots. "It was painfully phony," he says. Subsequent visits to Hog Ranch by police brought charges ranging from possession of illegal game trophies and stolen property to violation of immigration laws.

On June 12 the pressure heated up. The *Kenya Times* ran a front page story claiming that Beard had used Kamante over the years for his own gain. "The young American entrepreneur was interested in the ready-made Kamante that had already been created by Karen Blixen," reported the paper. "He was all out to exploit Kamante's fame and knowledge of Kenya and Africa. His ideals of living with Kamante in an unspoilt environment might have been realized if Kamante himself clearly understood the white man's intentions."

The story was based on interviews with the same family members intent on having fifty percent of Hog Ranch for their own. It accused Beard of inheriting Hog Ranch from Karen Blixen, who had intended half for Beard and half for Kamante. It also claimed that Beard had not shared profits from the book they had worked on together. The paper repeated these charges despite the fact that Beard had assured the reporter—who came to Hog Ranch and interviewed him accompanied by a dozen "assistants"—that the first accusation was totally wrong and that he had not made a penny off the book. He added that he had supported Kamante and his family since 1962. (Kamante, totally paralyzed, was in no position to defend himself or either of his white friends. He died on June 29.)

On June 19, the *Kenya Times* attacked again, running another front-page article intended to finish off Beard. This one was the sad story of Hassan Geddy, Iman's husband, who claimed—ten years after the fact—that Beard had "stolen" his wife from him. "He broke our marriage," he told the newspaper, "and tried to murder me."

Hassan claimed that Beard had come to him at the Hilton where he worked in 1975 and said, "'I hear you are married to that beautiful girl called Iman.' I said yes and we got talking as he explained to me the immense potential my wife had in the United States as a model, how we were wasting our time and opportunities in Kenya and how he could make us millionaires if we went with him to the States." He went on to say that Beard promised them both fame and riches. He claimed to have followed Beard and Iman to New York, where the photographer encouraged him to go home because it wouldn't look good if the press found out Iman was married. Finally, he claimed Beard threatened to kill him if he didn't leave New York.

Beard told the paper then the same story he maintains today. "I didn't know Hassan . . . I had never seen him, never set eyes on him." Iman was in Kenya soon after the story came out, and she vehemently denied her husband's version in interviews, telegrams, and public statements. Hassan's motivation was apparently double-barreled, aimed at kneecapping Beard as well as making a case that he should be compensated by his now wealthy ex-wife.

This year of nonstop trouble sent Beard into an emotional spiral. When it became apparent that it wasn't just Francis Kimani he was up against, but forces with the backing of the president's office, the charges against him looked increasingly serious even though they were badly flawed. His defense was coordinated by his New York–based manager Peter Riva. High-powered Americans, once again including Jackie Onassis, made appeals to the State Department on his behalf; France's Prime Minister Jacques Chirac and even Francis Bacon wrote letters to the government of Kenya deploring the charges.

Iman, model Janice Dickinson, and Princess Elizabeth of Yugoslavia came to Nairobi to be with the increasingly frustrated and angry Beard. The advice that Beard move out of Hog Ranch in November came from the State Department, based on the theory that "the best way to end a witch-hunt is to kill the witch." The CIA advised him that rather than allow his trial to become an international incident they would "lift him out" of Kenya under a cloak of mystery. They gave him a password; if he

166

Beard and Elizabeth of Yugoslavia
in the Intercontinental Hotel, Nairobi, 1985.
During a period of raids on Hog Ranch,
and trials, Beard moved into the hotel.
Here he types bail applications.

even use her real house in the movie. The Blixens' home was too small for the production so instead they used the opulent home of Mama Ngina, first president Jomo Kenyatta's widow. Meryl Streep was good, but the whole thing looked like a plastic, California-ized Hallmark card with slight movement. The wildlife and the natives were used like shiny props. I could barely stay awake through it. If Karen Blixen were alive and saw that film she'd kill herself."

Perhaps Beard's greater disappointment was that he had let the film rights to the book slip through his hands, rights granted him by Karen Blixen's family and foundation. Over the years he had made occasional progress toward assembling a film based on the book. "I had recorded her family talking about her . . . Mick Jagger had offered to do the original soundtrack," he says. It goes without saying that Beard's *Out of Africa* would have been much different from Sydney Pollack's.

He stands up from the campfire and enters the mess tent. After ten minutes digging through a filing cabinet buried in a corner under a pile of newspapers and magazines, he reemerges with a fading photocopy of a letter, dated December 6, 1967, from the Rungstedlund Foundation, executors of Blixen's estate.

Here's what it says: "The author Isak Dinesen (Karen Blixen) donated her literary estate to the Rungstedlund Foundation, established in 1958 and conformed and approved by the King of Denmark and the Danish Ministry for Cultural Affairs . . . of special importance is *Out of Africa,* which is not only a great work of art, but also a book with a message to humanity. Plans for filming this book were brought forward already in the author's lifetime. She herself could not see how this could be done. After her death several film projects based on the book have been laid before us . . . after having acquainted ourselves with the plans outlined by Peter Beard, author of *The End of the Game,* who was a personal acquaintance of the late Baroness Blixen, we have become convinced of the fact that if it be at all possible to carry the artistic values and the message of *Out of Africa* safely over into cinematographic form, he is the artist to do so. . . . This is not a task to be accomplished on a tight time-schedule. It calls for patience. . . . But it is important that the work should be begun as soon as possible . . . because the conditions on which it is contingent become more and more difficult to establish with each day. . . . We therefore want to recommend most warmly the work that Peter Beard has in mind, which can be expected to result in material suited for a motion picture as well as for Television. . . . If it is rendered possible for him to set about this work in the way which he has visualized, we would want to keep in contact with him and to give him all the support that we can in the shape of information and photographs from Isak Dinesen's African years, and we shall not grant television or film rights in connection with *Out of Africa* to others while work on these plans is in progress."

The letter is signed by three board members, including Blixen's longtime aide-de-camp, Clara Svendsen.

Despite such apparent blanket authority, the struggle for the rights to the book only heightened after Beard received the Rungstedlund letter. In 1968 a Hollywood producer named Sidney Blaustein offered the Blixen family $150,000 for the rights (Beard had put down nothing but his good name). "The foundation people called me up," says Beard, "and I said give it to him, he'll never be able to make the movie. I'll call mine 'End of the Game' or 'Longing for Darkness,' what do I care." In the 1970s Columbia Pictures offered the foundation $200,000 for the *Out of Africa* rights, promising Nicolas Roeg as the director. Again they were granted. (Beard: "Nick Roeg was a great friend of mine, we'd worked together in Africa, we'd hung out in London and at Studio 54, but he had an awful script. The truth about Africa is very elusive and hard for outsiders to pin down—I knew he couldn't make the film with that corny script.") Finally, when Universal and Sydney Pollack offered big money for rights to the book, Beard knew it was forever out of his hands.

In 1984 Beard read Pollack's script and they talked about him serving as the Nairobi-based technical adviser to the film. Before a deal could be struck, however, a competitor for the job badmouthed Beard to the director—spreading stories about arrests, drug use at Hog Ranch, and other *fitina*—and he was not hired. "At first I wanted to help," says Beard, "but it was also clear they wanted to do a plastic, Hollywood film. Up until then I'd been a great follower of Pollack's, he'd done a lot of great movies. But this one was just too phony."

What irritated Beard was that Pollack didn't understand Blixen or any part of her Africa. A German journalist staying at Hog Ranch was granted an interview with Pollack during filming. He asked the director why he was making the movie, and his reply was typically Hollywood: "Because I bought the rights." "The guy then asked him what the title meant, if he knew anything about the book," remembers Beard. "Pollack didn't know the title came from Pliny ['Always something new and strange, out of Africa . . .']. All he knew was that he'd bought it and had Robert Redford to play Finch Hatton."

Despite Beard's revulsion, the film went on to win seven Academy Awards. The result? Blixenmania. In 1986, the year after the movie swept the Oscars, the number of visitors to Kenya jumped from 541,000 to 604,000. A thriving industry sprang up around her life, her coffee farm,

Iman getting a lesson in lion training for her role in *Out of Africa*, filmed in Karen, Kenya, 1986

her lover, and the Ngong Hills, including but hardly limited to "Out of Africa" cocktail and champagne picnics, horseback treks through what was once her 6,000-acre spread, walking safaris in the Ngong Hills, and pilgrimages to Finch Hatton's grave. Mbogani was renovated and turned into a museum. Mahogany was stripped of white paint and furnishings were tracked down, many of which had been sold at auction. Universal Studios donated props, including a cuckoo clock, an old typewriter, Redford's hat, and Streep's riding britches. History and celluloid myth were so confused that Streep's boots today elicit the same reaction from visitors as the pair of lamps that Blixen used to set out at night to signal Finch Hatton that she was home.

· · · · · · · · · ·

If the late eighties were highlighted by *fitina,* a pair of personal relationships saved the decade for Beard. The first was his marriage to Najma Khanum, daughter of a Kenyan high-court judge whom he had met in May 1985, just prior to the onset of his nightmare legal problems. The second was the birth of his daughter, Zara, three years later.

He and Najma were introduced by a mutual friend at the Norfolk Hotel. Before the end of the afternoon she had agreed to let Beard take her photograph. She knew him merely by reputation, though she had a vague memory of seeing a picture of him inside a crocodile's mouth in *Newsweek.* At the time he was married (to Tiegs) and known around Nairobi as a playboy and partier, hardly the upstanding Moslem Najma's parents had in mind for her.

Before that first weekend was out Beard had convinced her to help him write a letter to the Kenya National Museums (then run by Richard Leakey), decrying plans to turn the Blixen home into little more than a museum for "farm implements." Soon Najma was doing research for Beard and Iman, who were planning to start a clothing company. When Najma began spending nights at Hog Ranch, her father sent the local constables out to retrieve her. They arrived, somewhat sheepishly, with sirens wailing and guns at hand. Her father then kept her at home behind locked doors for six weeks. Apparently what her father knew of Beard, he didn't like.

Najma was twenty-five at the time. Her mother—the descendant of Afghani nobility—was Beard's age. Her father had come to Kenya as a barrister from England. His first clients were Mau Mau rebels; eventually he was appointed a high-court judge by Kenya's President Moi. Najma and her siblings led a very sheltered childhood in Nairobi. They were taken to the cinema by car and driver, and their protective parents allowed them few freedoms. ("Although my parents' house was full of academics, diplomats, politicians, and a variety of others, they feared we would be

172

Najma Beard

contaminated by the hoi polloi.") She was sent off to schools in London, Belgium, and Germany before returning to Kenya.

In an effort to cure her of her fixation with Beard, the judge sent his daughter to see the director of the Nairobi Hospital. "The doctor was a pretty nice guy and knew that Naj was totally sane," says Beard. The psychiatrist pronounced her fit, but encouraged her to placate her angry father. Eventually she was escorted to Nairobi Airport and put on a plane for Heidelberg, where her father's brother lived. She had two hundred pounds, which she promptly paid a cabdriver in Germany to mail a letter to Beard's friend Gillies Turle letting them know she was safe. On receipt of her note advising him of her whereabouts, Beard flew to Heidelberg to join her. There he presented her with a thirty-page letter professing undying admiration and love. (Coincident or not, in 1913 when Bror Blixen was in Africa and his soon-to-be-wife Karen still in Denmark, he sent a thirty-page safari journal to her full of photographs, bloodstains, and misspellings.)

Borrowing $10,000 from Francis Bacon, the runaway pair fled Germany for London and then New York. Najma had never been to the States before. When they arrived, they were welcomed home to a Studio 54 party attended by three hundred of Beard's friends. Beard was locked in a custody battle with Tiegs over the house in Montauk, so initially the couple lived with friends and for a few days in a borrowed van. The Tiegs-Beard divorce was final on September 25, 1985, and he and Najma eloped December 21. To this day Beard has not met his father-in-law.

Exotic in appearance, verbally feisty, and of patrician breeding, Najma is a good match for Beard. She rarely shrinks from challenging his more outlandish theorizing, yet is simultaneously one of his biggest supporters. "What people don't understand about Peebs, the reason he rails so much, is because he cares. He cannot stand to see the place he loves destroyed with such arrogance and disregard."

THIRTEEN

. . . .

White men always destroy what they claim to love. We are shooting
it, felling it, making way for farms. And now that we have slain so much,
mown down so many millions of head of game over the years, we start
societies for the preservation of the remaining relics, because Africans, free
now, feel it is their turn, and want to shoot what has been left to them.

— GERALD HANLEY,
Warriors and Other Strangers

On the Wild-deer-ness, Silly Sentimentalists, and (Over) Population

When are we going to wake up and realize we only have
one habitat, and that we're destroying it faster and faster each day.

— BEARD

Before Beard arrived, Kenya's big-game sanctuaries were one of the wonders
of the world. By the early sixties much of the country's fabled game had
been pushed into massive preserves intended to attract millions of tourists
with their Kodak Instamatics and foreign currencies. The entire continent
was being pawned off as a giant outdoor zoo. According to the scientists—
and Beard wholeheartedly concurred—there was a mammoth problem
with those game preserves: They were totally artificial constructs, set up
with complete disregard for the responsibilities of viable management and
the basic principles of population dynamics. The animals inside the
preserves were reproducing like rabbits, ravaging the environment, and
then slowly starving to death. Today in Kenya conservation is little more
than what Beard labels "a large-scale pet-keeping operation" and a precar-
ious one at that. A fast-expanding human population has taken the greatest
toll. "Human islands in a sea of elephants changed to increasingly small
islands of elephants in a sea of people," is how Dick Laws describes the
changes.

"Populations expand . . . land does not."
—Teddy Roosevelt, 1915.
1977 view of elephants in Amboseli,
which is today a ruined landscape.

Beard came to Africa for the wildlife (or the "wild-deer-ness," as he put it), anxious to live a life of high adventure. But things went awry: The twentieth century caught up with Kenya. Tribes were coalescing into nations; roads were being built, fences were cropping up, towns and cities were spreading everywhere. The old Africa was vanishing forever, and it was Beard's misfortune—or fate—to be present at its passing. He became obsessed with the costs of modernity, with the ugliness and desolation that were the price of the Dark Continent's enlightenment.

He has remained faithful to his calling, committed to drumming home his concerns by documenting the disaster in his adopted home. His special interest—the fate of African wildlife—has become his passion, and he is bolstered today by the knowledge that the very message he has been shouting for the past three decades is now being echoed around Kenya, even as the wildlife scene decays faster and faster. While there are optimists here and there, the correlation between what has happened to East Africa's wildlife and man's own future has been undeniably established, a theme Beard has been trying urgently to communicate. (Remember the subtitle of Beard and Graham's Lake Rudolf book: "The Mingled Destinies of Crocodiles and Men.") There are glimmers of hope, however. As the 1990s began, Beard had a particularly enlightening experience, one that gave him renewed optimism about Africa's future.

He'd heard about a wildlife management success story being conducted in the middle of the Ovahimba desert in Damaraland, on the Skeleton Coast of Namibia. Under the supervision of noted South African scientists Garth Owen-Smith and Margaret Jacobsohn, herds of elephants and rhinos were actually on the increase. Beard had to see it for himself.

In advance of his trip to southern Africa he convinced the German *Forbes* to run an eight-page collage of what he found. He was excited by the successes he hoped to discover and selfishly hoped that by producing an optimistic story about how wildlife management can work, he might influence what he calls the "sentimental" fundraisers back in Kenya on how they might "rethink their hopelessly short-term, beggars' positions." "It was to be an insider's view of the looming conservation scene," says Beard, "no pulled punches, just the truth. They wanted optimism and they advanced me $16,000."

Beard spent seventy-eight days, hosted by Owen-Smith and Jacobsohn, driving hundreds of miles under very harsh conditions. Because his books are widely known around Africa he was granted great entrée and met with wardens and administrators at parks across South Africa and Namibia. "They like me down there," he says, "because I'm into 'management.' People down there groan at the way East Africa has treated its wildlife."

In Namibia, Owen-Smith and Jacobsohn have had success simply by involving the rural people in conservation, an approach they've dubbed regional participation, or localism. By integrating the aspirations and needs of black subsistence farmers with conservation priorities they've been able to teach the farmers that saving the animals is more profitable than killing them. Beard went with them to one of their pilot projects, in which Himba and Herero tribesmen are reaping the benefits.

"In the Ovahimba Desert poaching has been reduced to nil," says Beard, "because the poachers—often local inhabitants—now have a direct stake in the game. The answer lies neatly within the problem. Money flows in from tourists who come to see nature preserved, and from game products (horns, skins, tusks) harvested from a well-managed population. At last wildlife has been allowed to pay for itself, instead of relying on sentimental charity schemes."

Beard visiting
Kenya Safari Club
orphanage for wildlife,
1983

As well as a learning experience, the trip was a rich photo expedition for Beard, who felt renewed by the success of his fellow conservationists. He photographed tribesmen dehorning rhinos, a task that makes perfect economic and management sense but that would never be done in Kenya for the hue and cry of the sentimentalists. In Namibia the horns are sold, the money going to help support the parks and the surrounding community. As for the dehorned rhino, he now lives without fear of being poached.

Beard also spent long days and nights photographing the Himba and Herero tribesmen in Damaraland, documenting the last vestiges of an abundant, original wildlife. This scene was as rich and as real as the days he spent photographing the Turkana, Samburu, and Merille at Lake Rudolf in the sixties, reminding him of those good old days he so missed. "These people are so genuine, totally unlike anything you see elsewhere today. Real evolutionary characters, even more so than the Turkana, a tribe I knew quite well."

"The whole trip rekindled a long-lost affinity, optimism and belief in the soul-cleansing ways of the Old Africa," he wrote upon his return. "It was the indescribable Africa I saw again, a wilderness with simplicity, existential isolation and primordial authenticity. All that has been lost in our ravaged world." At one point during his visit he took leave of his hosts for three days and wandered by himself into the desert, carrying little more than his camera. He walked during the day and slept in caves at night—a solitary effort aimed at renewing his dwindling contact with such wilderness.

As he worked, he had his films developed, sixty-five rolls in all. Before leaving Namibia he began to plot the collage he would deliver to *Forbes.* The magazine intended to mix photographs of the two most primitive peoples he'd met—the Herero of Namibia and the Turkana of Kenya—to illustrate their similarities and disparities in the nineties.

"It was a unique opportunity, to put wild creativity and ecological realities into a business magazine," says Beard. "People don't want to read any more of the trumped-up statistics, they want to see the thing in pictures or collage. Basically they wanted to see a piece drawn from thirty-five years of experience, all I've seen, 'without the boredom of the conveyance.' It was a unique chance, a foot in the door to provide a new kind of report."

On Saturday, March 31, 1990, a few minutes before April Fools day, Beard readied to board a Lufthansa plane from Nairobi to New York to deliver his finished collages. Filled with negatives, slides, contact sheets, and Cibachromes, his portfolio was taken at the gate because it was too large to be carried on. It was sent back to the check-in counter, where it was mistakenly tagged and sent to Rhodesia. Despite days spent searching the lost-luggage tombs below Frankfurt International Airport, the portfolio—containing all those negatives, slides, contact sheets, and Cibachromes—was never found.

· · · · · · · · · · ·

Despite the loss—and the headache of the lawsuits that followed as he attempted to be compensated for his lost artwork—the trip to southern Africa revived Beard's belief that wildlife management could work, that maybe it wasn't too late. But his optimism deflates whenever he considers the "management" steps being currently taken in Kenya. Since his Namibia experience, he has joined the increasingly loud, global debate over the various wildlife management styles being used across Africa. These days it is his favorite topic of conversation. And nothing sets him off more than the widely publicized ivory ban, encouraged by his old friend Richard Leakey, head of Kenya's Wildlife Services.

Elephants,
Mt. Kilimanjaro,
Amboseli,
1988

Leakey was appointed to the KWS job in 1988. When he took over the parks were in a shambles, losing a thousand elephants a year to poachers. Rangers were printing up their own admission tickets and pocketing the money. Low-level clerks drove Mercedeses, and gate guards were skimming off ticket receipts. Rangers were still shooting elephants and rhinos from the back of park vehicles, with guns bought for them with conservation group money. For a bribe they often looked the other way when Somalis poached. The lowest-paid employees were stealing new equipment and anything else they could get their hands on.

Since taking over Leakey has lopped twenty-five hundred employees from the department, stopped much of the corruption, and has raised a reported $240 million from mostly Western donors and agencies. The money is to be spent on his vision of how to run what remains of Kenya's wildlife. Based largely on his money-raising skills, Leakey has won the support of his government as well as that of big-money donors and wildlife groups around the world.

I visited Leakey in his Nairobi national park office, just a few miles from Hog Ranch. He was polite and politic, crossing his feet atop a glass-topped coffee table as we talked. Out the window stretched the five-thousand-acre park that abuts the city of three million.

Leakey claims his biggest accomplishment has been convincing the Convention on International Trade in Endangered Species (CITES) to adopt the worldwide ban on the sale of ivory, which has essentially killed any legitimate market for tusks and rhino horns. He claims it has also ended poaching in Kenya, thus saving the lives of untold elephants. In truth, while poaching has slowed, it is in part due to the fact that most of the old elephants with valuable tusks were killed by poachers during the 1980s. And the ivory business that still exists has gone underground. Increasing numbers of experts agree that the ban is not a long-term solution. (Or in the words of a recent report by Ian Parker and Alistair Graham, "The cessation of ivory hunting would no more stop the process than aspirin cure the cause of headaches.")

In fact, as Beard likes to point out, Kenya and Leakey find themselves in a trap of their own making. Much better known for his fossil finds of humanity's ancestors, Leakey stands accused of ill-informed grandstanding for the sake of Western dollars. By promoting tourism over sound wildlife management he has collected scads of money, but now his hands are tied. In certain of Kenya's parks there are too many elephants. This is particularly true of the southern park of Amboseli, where roughly eight hundred live in an area too small to sustain them. The herd desperately needs to be culled in order to ensure survivability for the habitat. The tree cover has

given way to savanna, pushing out the giraffes, monkeys, and bushbucks that thrived on the old vegetation, but there is no place left for Amboseli's elephants to go. Knowledgeable sources say Leakey will have to start culling or else experience the same catastrophic failure witnessed in Tsavo in the early seventies. However, Leakey is on record as insisting he will never authorize the shooting of an elephant, a promise he has made over and over to his big money givers in return for their donations.

Leakey is known as a master at press manipulation and has received notice around the world for his burning of confiscated ivory. His biggest acclaim came in 1989, when he torched twelve metric tons of confiscated ivory worth more than $3 million. It made for splendid theater: Special effects pros painted the two thousand tusks in the eighteen-foot-high pyre with highly flammable glue. Beneath them was laid an abundance of dry kindling, to be stoked by a grid of gas pipes injecting sixty gallons of gasoline and diesel fuel into the mass. When the pile was matched—by Leakey—President Moi stood by, carved ivory *rungu* in hand, under an idyllic blue sky, watching thick black smoke curl off the burning pyre. Beard was present for the burning, photographing it for *Paris Match.*

The ivory ban came about in part because selfishly motivated donors saw their playground—primarily Kenya—being left elephantless. One reason for the continued decimation of the elephant population was that ivory had simply become too valuable. The motive behind Leakey's support of the ivory ban was to devalue ivory by making it illegal to buy or sell, but others felt that taking "white gold" off the market would simply increase its value because of its new rarity.

How valuable had ivory become? In 1970 it was selling for $2.30 a pound on world markets in Brussels, Hong Kong, and Tokyo, and a decade later it was fetching $70. The rhino horn is even more expensive, selling for up to $300 in the Middle East, where it is carved into handles for traditional daggers or ground into a fine powder for medicinal use. This increase in value explains the booming growth of high-tech poachers, many armed with AK-47s and sophisticated radios.

As a result of Leakey's fervent lobbying (backed by powerful western allies), 105 of 110 nations party to CITES agreed to ban the raw ivory trade. Only Malawi and Zambia refused, as did three nations with healthy herds of elephants: South Africa, Zimbabwe, and Botswana. Tough conservation programs in those countries have protected a valuable and sustainable natural resource based, in part, on the value of ivory on the market. An ivory trade ban, they argued, would undermine that success. In most nations, however, the ban has had its intended effect, causing ivory prices, hence poaching, to fall.

Richard Leakey
at the ivory burn,
Nairobi,
1991

181

Since its adoption, the ban has earned Leakey the wrath of many of his peers across the continent, particularly in southern Africa, where tusks from the managed killing of elephants are stacked unsold. Those who have worked in the wildlife trade all their lives insist that Leakey—who knew a lot about bones but precious little about live animals when he took the job—has hurt them by pushing for the ban. Noel Brown, director of the United Nations Environmental Programme, labeled the ban "obscene."

In the countries of southern Africa, as Beard witnessed most success-fully in Namibia, the approach to wildlife is more down-to-earth, more like cattle ranching. Although it offends some wildlife purists, these countries see the animals as cash crops, much like cattle. Closely managed herds remain stable, but only because hunters are sold expensive permits to cull them. The ivory, meat, hides, bone, and even hair are then sold and the profits put back into game management and local economies. In Zimbabwe hunting safaris bring in $15 million a year; the sale of ivory, another $1 million. Countries like Zimbabwe have figured out how to use wildlife to pay for itself. In Kenya they're still trying desperately (and futilely) to keep the animals "wild," in a "natural" setting. But it's too late for that approach.

Leakey understands that fallout from the ivory ban could be his downfall, certainly his public relations ruination, especially if the ban encourages a permanent "anti-ivory" marketplace. If that happens, it will forever destroy the potential for supporting wildlife through the sale of wildlife products. He also realizes that Kenya's fast-growing population may make protecting wildlife an afterthought, since it is likely that Kenya's parklands will soon be filled with men, women, and children, not wild animals. Nevertheless, Leakey argues that in Kenya that won't happen: "I think the importance of tourism to this country is so clear that the govern-ment won't allow tourist-based industry—wildlife—to be eroded by the human population." He then implies that Kenya's people should learn to live anywhere else, even the desert, before taking over the parks.

Perhaps Leakey's most incendiary prediction regards the potential effects of AIDS on Kenya's long-term future. "Population growth in Kenya will come down because we do have a very serious AIDS problem," he says. "We will see a very significant loss of life." Kenya reports seventeen thousand deaths from the plague and more than a hundred thousand infected. Statistics are very hard to confirm here, but the truth is that many, many more are infected. Leakey firmly believes the disease may ultimately prove beneficial as a population reducer, a heavy-handed philosophy heard increasingly from both white and black leaders across Africa, *though rarely spoken publicly.*

"The cost in human life will be very high," says Leakey, "not only on the HIV positive but on the medical services, which affect things like infant mortality and the ability of government to provide even basic services for such things as influenza and chicken pox. While not a happy scenario, it is not necessarily as gloomy as some forecast."

Plague or no plague, Leakey expects to be on to new challenges soon and says he definitely won't stick around to see all of the $240 million spent. "I think even two more years in this job would be too long. It's a job one cannot possibly enjoy, given the stress, strain, hassle, responsibility. If I can raise the money and establish an institution that has its own life, I'll move on." Whenever he leaves the job, says one critic, what he'll leave behind is the equivalent of having "built his ego-serving castle on quicksand."

. . . .

Not everyone in Kenya is as pessimistic as Beard. In fact, a pioneering brand of optimism has excited Beard recently, the potential for what he describes as "entrepreneurial" wildlife management. To illustrate, he takes me to meet Calvin Cottar, the twenty-eight-year-old son of Beard's old bushmate, Glen.

Calvin represents another possible future for Kenya's wildlife. A fourth-generation white Kenyan, he is a kind of neo-bushman, more likely to carry a briefcase than a gun and to spend more time formulating fresh approaches to utilizing Kenya's game than tracking it across the plains. "Two years ago," says Calvin, "I thought photo safaris were my future. To own my own safari company was my dream. Now I've matured."

We talk over dinner in Calvin's tent, which is set up on his father's Karen estate. The meal is vegetarian; he says he rarely eats meat. Past are the days when his dad's generation feasted nightly on gazelle, buffalo ribs, eland, and impala. Calvin is proud of his shift in direction and of the fact that his dad and he don't see eye to eye on what needs to be done to preserve some semblance of the Kenya that first attracted his great-grandfather in the 1890s. He is driven by the fact that Kenya's wildlife management, or lack of same, makes the country, in his words, the "laughingstock" of Africa.

Beard has known Calvin since he was knee-high and still calls him by his childhood nickname of "Curly"—an odd moniker for a brawny, six-foot-three-inch man. Many of his childhood friends have given up on Kenya and moved south to Zimbabwe, South Africa, or Namibia, where wildlife management has been better implemented, where there are still some good bush jobs left. The consensus is that efforts at managing wildlife in Kenya have been a failure, adopted too late, in part because of greedy

tour operators and professional hunting operations (including, Calvin admits, his own family). The old school got used to "taking, taking, taking," says Calvin. They gave too little back, to either the locals or their communities, contributing to the "game" ending. "They had no foresight," he says, "and now we're paying the penalty."

His hope, using his family's good name, is to open doors and try to mimic in Kenya some of the better programs working successfully in other countries: game ranching, hunting on private lands, and the export of specially bred game. He's looking for partners, venture capital, and government aid, but he acknowledges that it is a hard sell.

Calvin's biggest roadblock is simply getting his message heard. He knows the media and money-raising machines are dominated by "bunny

White hunters' annual meeting at Glen Cottar's camp, 1983. Cottar is at bottom right.

huggers" who spend their time and energy on saving a *few* animals while ignoring the big picture, the future. He readily admits that the pleas for monetary support from wildlife "orphanages" are better heard than his, which promotes game ranching, or sustained yield harvesting.

As we talk Beard points out that Africa's biggest problem has long been balancing her natural resources against the needs of humans. African habitats are ecologically brittle and liable to deteriorate rapidly. Conservation measures must therefore safeguard habitats and resources and ensure the best land usage. Game farming may be the key to this goal. Game produces more meat per acre and with less damage to the land than domestic stock. Wild game is also more capable of traveling farther from water, thus utilizing more land in times of drought.

Calvin predicts that Richard Leakey's biggest donors—the World Bank and USAID—are soon going to insist that proper management techniques be a condition of any donation. What that means is that Kenya Wildlife Services will one day soon be forced to get behind ideas like game ranching, maybe even culling, regardless of the promises made by its director.

· · · · · · · · · · ·

Despite glimpses of optimism, Beard remains resolute in his belief that the end of the game is truly near. "The play period is over," he often reminds. It will take a lot of hard work to save the wild game that remains in Kenya, and most days Beard doesn't think it's worth the effort.

While he has known Leakey for twenty-five years and has a grudging respect for him, Beard thinks he's definitely on the wrong course. "He continues to talk about contraception, fences, improved technology, more manpower . . . it's all hot air. Africa's five hundred and seventeen million population will be more than a billion in less than twenty-five years. Famine will increase, habitat will decrease, wildlife will disappear. Tourism is a ruinous joke [though it brings seven hundred thousand people and about $10 million in revenues to Kenya each year]. My only advice is see it now before it's gone.

"Leakey's basic problem is that he simply doesn't tell the truth. Elephants are still being poached, population pressures are increasing, tour groups are attacked, yet mysteriously the newspapers don't report it. He continues to talk about fencing all of the country's parks, even while elephants and humans alike are taking electric fences apart."

Beard rarely has anything good to say about the western money-raising agencies, whose raison d'être he calls "heroism through money." "Their problem is that in order to raise money they lie and make promises like 'In our world there can be no justification for killing elephants.' That's simply not honest and the same old sentimental thinking that destroyed Tsavo."

On this score, Beard is joined by a growing chorus of conservationists. Esmond Bradley Perry Martin III, an American who has lived in Langata almost as long as Beard has and whose expertise is ivory markets, compares over-zealous preservationists to anti-abortion groups. "They are increasingly well-organized and well-financed," he says. "In the long run they present more danger to wildlife than they offer for protection."

Ron Thomson, a South African biologist, sides with Beard and Martin in decrying the growth of "Save the Elephant" campaigns. He maintains in his recent book, *Killing with Kindness,* that "those people who recognize the danger signs should not simply hang their heads. . . . They must find ways and means to combat this dangerous development because otherwise the natural world will be utterly destroyed by such subjective sentiment."

"All I am trying to do," says Beard, "is bring to people's attention visual evidence, the truth about so-called conservation. And the truth is damned simple. Of course everything is changing fast—the righteous hue and cry goes up in a direct ratio to the degree it is too late. Things are racing now . . . screaming into the future. But I hate the word pessimism . . . I'm trying to be realistic, dealing in the truth. People around me who aren't realistic are inadvertent liars or con men.

"There are solutions: Can't we encourage the government to change those tax benefits for extra children to tax penalties? Can't we elect leaders who have a feeling for our one and only habitat? Let's make them realize we care about the fouling of our one and only nest and *won't take it anymore.* Zero population growth is 2.1 children per family. That's the bottom line. That is the ultimate solution.

"Forget trying to save the rhinos, forget the elephants. Get this absolutely straight: We are now fighting to save ourselves and our once diverse way of life. You think I'm joking, I am not. I have seen this place fall apart in a mere twenty years. People aren't operating with overall intelligence; we're not educating ourselves to survive, we are not electing leaders who are aware of the depths of the problem. The problem is us, our population. We're a cancer on earth, taking it over like a disease." Kenya's population, the fastest-growing in the world, is currently estimated to be somewhere between twenty-five and thirty million; it is expected to grow to more than sixty million by the year 2020.

Beard's opinions have earned him both followers and detractors in Kenya, each with varied opinions of their own regarding the message bearer. One midnight we find ourselves in the comfortable Langata living room of John and Angela Sutton, both of whom have known Beard for

thirty years. John is the president of Ker & Downey. A handful of his employees are over, and talk is of the future of their profession. The safari business has slowed mightily since the Gulf War; the gathering is particularly incensed that American ambassador Smith Hempstone continues to issue *"unsafe to travel"* warnings.

After Beard says goodnight, John Sutton remarks that he seems like "a new man" and credits Zara. "I've never seen him like that, so sedate," he says. This crowd of second- and third-generation white Kenyans, though similar to him in age, regards Beard as having a certain air of celebrity and simultaneously as a child, albeit a smart, precocious one. The next morning Beard talks about how his host and friends have changed, too.

One-year-old mountain gorilla in Rwanda forest. The forest is cut back annually to accommodate humans.

"These guys used to be the kings of Kenya. John and his brother Frank used to host annual barbecues up on their estate in Mweiga, where everyone who was anyone in white Kenya turned out. Over the years John has played host to royalty, movie stars, tycoons. Now he's reduced to living in a suburb next to a tennis court, behind iron bars and guarded by barking dogs and *askari* [night watchmen], reduced to conducting photo or fishing safaris for the average Joe. For him and the others . . . it's over."

It is another morning begun basking in sunlight around a smoldering campfire. Beard reads the papers, periodically getting up to scratch and detick his favorite warthogs, Thaka, Jr. and Ol Laleggi. (After a good rub, he points out, your fingertips smell like bacon.) Finches and a tree squirrel feed on the pig's corn, a turaco sings in the trees. The Ngongs are masked by clouds, the green valley muted. The fire takes the chill off the morning.

To his credit, Beard is the first to admit he's not interested in becoming an expert of any kind, that he has always been more interested in knowing a little about a lot. "I'm not a conservationist, naturalist, biologist, scientist, or ecologist. I have no official position in this thing, but I do have eyes. I can see and can exercise common sense. It has never been my intention to suggest what should be done, but only to document what has been done." In some ways Beard is an artist dressed up in conservationist's clothing. While his photographs from the bush are unmatched, his ability with facts and figures is sometimes fraught with over-enthusiasm. Richly and fervently cynical, he and his message can be so negative, so repetitious, that they are like opposing magnets, turning lifelong pessimists into born-again hopefuls.

You don't have to go far in Kenya to find critics of Beard and his singular brand of ecology. Elephant expert Iain Douglas-Hamilton's property adjoins Hog Ranch; he once labeled Beard a "scavenger." (It's a story Beard actually relishes. He and Douglas-Hamilton were at the site of a plane crash that had killed the pilot. Beard was collecting zebra-striped pieces of the plane for his diary, provoking Douglas-Hamilton's wrath. "You're just a scavenger," he declared.) Daphne Sheldrick once hurled *The End of the Game* across a crowded room with disgust, branding it "the worst thing that ever happened to Kenyan conservation."

Even his friends wish he were occasionally more contrite. Calvin Cottar suggests that "if Peter were just less extreme, he'd be a power here. But he's too much for people, too smart perhaps, and they won't take the time to listen." Dick Laws wishes Beard wouldn't "trip over the edges" so much. "But he's done his job. Even if people don't agree with him, he certainly tends to make people think." Filmmaker Bert Van Munster contends that "everybody who takes the effort to know him loves him. But most people are against him before they meet him, based on his reputation."

Beard admits he is "heavily into beating a dead horse." In fact, he prefers that the "do-gooders," the "foolish sentimentalists," see him as a poisonous thorn in their sides. He is satisifed, too, that his long-held positions on Kenya's wildlife future have been accepted in most circles.

Beard and crowned eagle, 1987

That is perhaps the most difficult thing about Beard, and especially frustrating to his critics. For all his name calling and loose-cannon broadsides, at the soul of his diatribes and stinging rebukes lies the truth. He witnessed the once-lush landscape turn to barren wasteland. He was way ahead of many people in warning about the elephants and the trees and talking about the crises of a limited food base. While he may seem puerile to some, he remains a visionary of sorts. Too, he continues to attract an audience for his words and pictures in part because he remains one of the most charismatic people you'll ever spend time with.

No one has had more insight into Beard over the past decade than Gillies Turle, who has lived at Hog Ranch since 1982. A one-time British military man, Gillies came to Kenya as a bodyguard for a white cabinet minister in 1965. After the minister was assassinated (by an altitude bomb over the Ngong Hills), Turle ran safaris for Ker & Downey before opening an antiques store. He ran with the polo-playing set, married, had two kids, bought a house in the suburbs. With his move to Hog Ranch, he left that life far behind.

"For the first two years I lived here I couldn't understand a word Peter was saying," Turle says one day in the crow's nest office of his downtown Nairobi storefront. "I came from completely another world. The next two years I became a kind of Peter clone. In retrospect, I was probably quite embarrassing. But if you are into wine, women, song, negativity, criticism, and atheism, which I was at the time, you can have quite a good time with Peter.

"But on a trip to New York with Peter I met a woman and was going on and on, in a Peter-influenced rap, about how everything was finished, how man was destroying the world, et cetera. She stopped me and said, 'Well, if man destroys the world, he can rebuild it.' I thought about it, and she was right. I haven't been a total disciple of Peter's since."

Over the years Gillies has seen a variety of characters come and go at Hog Ranch. "Most come for the glitterati, the scene," he admits. "His real friends come to see a warmhearted, intelligent, often lonely man.

"He's a hard one to figure out. Though I sense he's troubled, he would never see a shrink. He's been to a psychiatric hospital and I think he knows too much and is deathly afraid of what he knows is 'up' there. In order to change, in order to be more optimistic or less abrasive, he'd have to knock

down all the walls of negativity and pessimism he's spent years building. He refuses to do that, for reasons most likely of self-preservation."

Beard's most loyal friends prefer to recall the kind, gentle Beard over the one who can viciously dress down busboys and cabdrivers. Carol Bell says he would do anything for a friend in trouble. She confesses, too, that Beard's abrasiveness often masks compassion. "People fail to see his kind side. When someone is in trouble, from the camp cook on up, he responds. But he keeps that side of himself well hidden.

"But if you want to only see the dark side of humankind, the underbelly of the world, that's all you will see. If you refocus, you'll see the good. Peter is intently focused on the bad, the rotten, the end of the game."

Beard takes some comfort in the fact that his passionate-if-pessimistic stand is shared by others he respects—Glen Cottar, for example, whom he met at Lake Naivasha in 1961 and worked and hunted with throughout the 1960s and 1970s. In many ways they are very different. Conservative and traditional, Cottar is one of the most respected men in Kenya. He doesn't always agree with Beard's positions, but counts him as a close friend.

One night at Glen's Karen home, the pair swap stories of old pals (many now dead) and wild nights in the bush, including one hilarious tale about a young Beard being hustled by Mary Hemingway at the counter of the New Stanley Hotel.

"The trouble is that the ruination is not limited to just Kenya, or even just Africa," says Cottar, the night rain pounding on the roof, "the whole world's going down the tubes." For once Beard has nothing to say.

Beard among an overpopulation of hippos in Lake Idi Amin, 1983. Massive hippo die-offs occur around every five years.

FOURTEEN

. . . .

I have to admit to constantly dire projections most of my life.
For centuries my kind of sunset/Armageddon/end-game doom clichés
have been tolerated, dismissed, and then life simply goes on.
Maybe something positive is going to happen . . .

BEARD

Like a Wildebeest in the Rain

The year I choose to visit Beard and East Africa is a particularly turbulent one. Most of Kenya's neighbors—Somalia, Sudan, Zaire, and Ethiopia— are wracked by civil unrest. Perhaps nothing illustrates better the turbulence shaking the continent than the goings-on in the two nations with Africa's strongest economies, South Africa and Kenya. Few can help but see the differences between the two: As South Africa has begrudgingly become more "free," Kenya has turned more paramilitary, more paranoid. Everyone agrees that the most critical problem in Kenya's immediate future is its swelling population, the fastest-growing in the world.

It is this unprecedented population explosion that bothers Beard more than anything about his adopted home. Though marginally more lush than its neighbors to the north—Ethiopia and the Sudan—Kenya is barely able to feed its current masses. Efforts to slow its 4 percent annual population increase are not working, and international expenditure on family planning is decreasing. Only 18 percent of women use modern contraception. (In a recent survey, one sixteen-year-old respondent, when asked how pregnancy occurs, replied, "We don't know since we haven't experienced it.") Even slim economic gains are negated by the demands of this burgeoning populace, 50 percent of which is under fifteen years of age.

While Kenya boils, Beard observes intently, content to clip the papers, polish his diaries, play with his daughter, and await any opportunity to get back into the bush. He remains as obsessive about the place today as when he arrived. He was a hopeless romantic then, and after thirty-six years of an on-again/off-again love affair, months living in the wilds, and the passing of many of his best African friends, after jail and lawsuits and *fitina* upon *fitina,* in many ways he is still a hopeless romantic. He longs desper-

Elui and Zara on
the Tiva River in 1991,
28 years after
Beard camped there

ately for the days when Africa was a comfortable, daring, inexpensive place for a remittance chum to escape to, not a place destined, like the vortex of a tornado, to be swept up and dumped into an aid- and AIDS-ridden disaster zone.

In many ways he has led a charmed life, yet the years have taken a physical toll. At fifty-five, he bears the weathered look of an aging movie actor or beach bum, his face often hidden behind Foster Grants. While he appears younger than he is, he's starting to wear down from years of bush life and hard living. His stomach is bad, and most mornings begin with a slug of Maalox. He prefers soft food because his teeth are literally worn away from incessant nighttime grinding (he claims he can't afford to see a dentist). He often cups a hand behind his right ear to hear and can no longer read without glasses. An unaccountable, incurable skin disease he calls "African crud" rashes his ankles. His age also shows in his references, many of which seem stuck in the 1960s ("Trudy [Truman Capote] and I used to split a bottle of Maalox every three or four days on the Stones tour"). Most photographs he takes are with a point-and-shoot automatic.

His life is filled with memories few can match. He's floated on Ari's yacht, married America's sweetheart, been searched out in the bush by Elia Kazan and Jessica Tandy, spent drunken weeks in the company of Francis Bacon, had a flat tire in Picasso's driveway, flown with the Stones, got Ava Gardner's blood for his diary, and dined with Karen Blixen and Andy Warhol. But those memories don't hold much flavor for him today. His obsessiveness, his intense focus on the future, nearly forces him to think only about what's ahead. "We're witnessing a disaster in the making, a human tragedy," he says, pointing north toward Mogadishu, the capital of Somalia. (This was mid-1991, months before world attention focused on the starvation and civil strife.) "Within my lifetime Kenya will fall." He intends to stick it out to whatever end, to continue documenting—in words, photographs, books, and films—his singular take on paradise.

The ever-increasing Kenyan population is touching Beard in a personal way. As the country nears implosion Hog Ranch is threatened by the swelling Nairobi populace. With his neighbors Beard has paid for a ten-foot-tall chain-link fence to wrap around a communal 150 acres, in an effort to protect what is left of the Mbgathi Forest from fast-encroaching development. But that is merely a Band-Aid. Roads are being surveyed and wells tested all around Hog Ranch. It is simply a matter of time before the expanding metropolis devours his once-private domain. Even the population of Hog Ranch is expanding. Currently more than thirty people—staff, relatives, and hangers-on—live on the grounds with Beard's grudging okay, including several grandchildren and great-grandchildren of Kamante.

Bathing
at Hog Ranch,
1987

Giving in to the inevitable, he is considering opening a treehouse museum, or Hog Ranch Bar and Grill, on the fringes of his property, a last stab at recreating some of the romance he feels has been lost here. "If things get really bad, we're on to the Congo, the Riviera of Africa," he says only half in jest.

One day, sitting on the porch of Hog Ranch's kitchen, I ask Beard if he ever thinks about leaving Kenya and not returning. Thoreau, after all, left Walden after just two years and never went back. Karen Blixen was in Kenya for seventeen years, then retreated when the going became too difficult. Beard has been here for more than thirty years. I wonder out loud if perhaps he has stayed in his paradise too long. Around every corner he has found the end of something and it has soured him.

"I disagree," he says when I suggest my theory. "I still think it is a great place, affording the greatest evolutionary perspective, the last chance to have your feet on the ground where we began. I think the thing to do is just sit back and enjoy it and know that it is the greatest show on earth. It might be the last show, but it's the biggest, the most exhilarating, phantasmagoric, riveting, devastating, great.

"Mostly I feel like the wildebeest out there in a rainstorm . . . you just put your head down and wait."

. . . .

Thankfully for sanity's sake, Beard stumbled upon a psychic savior of sorts a few years ago. A gleam of optimism shines on his days now, generated by his four-year-old daughter, Zara, who better than anyone before, is giving him an insight into himself. Friends suggest that because of her, Peter is growing up. He is so devoted to fatherhood that he takes time off from his litany of complaints and concerns to celebrate with her daily discoveries, rejoicing in her youth and freshness.

"Peebs?" She calls him by her mother's nickname for him.

"Yes, my little brat."

"Do you love me?"

"Oh, my little googie-boogie, of course I love you."

"Peebs—look at me—where do you live?"

"You know where, Boogs, we live on Hog Ranch, with all your piggies."

"But Peebs, can you tell me something, are you a good dancer?"

"You know that, too, Ga-ga. I'm a *bad* dancer, and a dirty, smelly, naughty boy as well."

"Oh, Daddy!"

Finally, Beard has a passion that doesn't dwell in darkness.

Beard and Zara,
Hog Ranch,
1991

Beard and Zara,
Hog Ranch,
1990

There are other reasons for optimism, as several big projects are in the offing as I ready to leave Hog Ranch. Plans for a Beard-hosted series of television specials featuring ecologically threatened locales around the globe are nearing finalization. An animated version of a book of children's stories based on *Zara's Tales from Hog Ranch* is in the works. A book featuring his photographs of Masai art, *The Hidden Art of the Masai,* has been published, and at least two other books are roaming around his head, one waiting to be published as soon as the current Kenya government falls. He has photo shoots booked in Botswana and Namibia for German and Italian *Vogue,* and two major shows—in Paris and Tokyo—are planned. "He's still frustrated when he's not busy," says Najma, "because he is bright, talented, he's got good ideas, and his vision has proven to be spot-on. But Peter has such high expectations—for himself and others—that it takes a lot to keep him happy."

Beard visits Karen House with his daughter, Zara, and tells her of his friendship with Karen Blixen, 1991.

Late one night, standing atop a Masai grave on Hog Ranch's border—a massive, ten-foot tall pile of rocks built centuries ago—we look out on a bright, moonlit night over the burgeoning suburb of Ongata Rongai. The horizon is aglow with house lights. "Can you imagine what this valley, this view, was like in Karen Blixen's day?" Beard wonders. When he first moved here there were no buildings in sight. He used to fall asleep to the roar of lions and the laugh of hyenas; buffaloes and lions walked through his property, and nightly visits from leopards were common. Tonight the peace is broken by the barking of dogs and the thump of the disco in the near distance.

Saddened by the jumble of twinkling lights and the pounding disco drumbeat, Beard admits he is nonetheless growing increasingly accepting of the future. "Every place changes, I understand that. But here it's been like a tornado. Now, it's almost over. My biggest whine is that the past thirty years have gone by so quickly."

Friends who visit Hog Ranch often carry away a romantic vision of Peter seated in front of his tent as the sun sets on the Ngong Hills. In their vision, he is seated beside his favorite Picasso painting, a fire is blazing, and in his hand is his favorite drink—a bullshot, made with vodka and beef bouillon. His diary is laid out on a table in front of him. As he works on it, until three or four in the morning, an occasional giraffe wanders up to him and, without glancing up, he takes a handful of bran from his pocket and holds it up for the giraffe to eat.

Today, far from Nairobi, I have the same image in my head, accompanied by the sound of robin chats, barking dogs, and Beard hollering for *baridi maziwa* (cold milk). On the one hand it is a comforting, peaceful image. On the other it is disconcerting. Though there is still a spark twinkling in his eyes, Beard is not smiling.

Those sunsets at Ngong have an atmosphere of
rest and content about them which I never realise
anywhere else. I believe I could die happily enough
at sunset there, looking up at the hills, with all
their lovely colours facing out above the
darkening belbelt near the forest.

— KAREN BLIXEN,
from a letter to Denys Finch Hatton